Self-Injury

by Toney Allman

LUCENT BOOKS

A part of Gale, Cengage Learning

Detroit • New York • San Francisco • New Haven, Conn • Waterville, Maine • London

LIBRARY OF CONGRESS CATALOGING-IN-PUBLICATION DATA

Allman, Toney.
  Self-injury / by Toney Allman.
      p. cm. -- (Hot topics)
  Includes bibliographical references and index.
  ISBN 978-1-4205-0552-8 (hardcover)
  1. Self-injurious behavior. 2. Self-mutilation. I. Title.
  RC569.5.S48A45 2011
  616.85'82--dc22
                                                         2010050010

Lucent Books
27500 Drake Rd.
Farmington Hills, MI 48331

ISBN-13: 978-1-4205-0552-8
ISBN-10: 1-4205-0552-1

Printed in the United States of America
2 3 4 5 6 7 15 14 13 12 11

CONTENTS

FOREWORD

Young people today are bombarded with information. Aside from traditional sources such as newspapers, television, and the radio, they are inundated with a nearly continuous stream of data from electronic media. They send and receive e-mails and instant messages, read and write online "blogs," participate in chat rooms and forums, and surf the Web for hours. This trend is likely to continue. As Patricia Senn Breivik, the former dean of university libraries at Wayne State University in Detroit, has stated, "Information overload will only increase in the future. By 2020, for example, the available body of information is expected to double every 73 days! How will these students find the information they need in this coming tidal wave of information?"

Ironically, this overabundance of information can actually impede efforts to understand complex issues. Whether the topic is abortion, the death penalty, gay rights, or obesity, the deluge of fact and opinion that floods the print and electronic media is overwhelming. The news media report the results of polls and studies that contradict one another. Cable news shows, talk radio programs, and newspaper editorials promote narrow viewpoints and omit facts that challenge their own political biases. The World Wide Web is an electronic minefield where legitimate scholars compete with the postings of ordinary citizens who may or may not be well-informed or capable of reasoned argument. At times, strongly worded testimonials and opinion pieces both in print and electronic media are presented as factual accounts.

Conflicting quotes and statistics can confuse even the most diligent researchers. A good example of this is the question of whether or not the death penalty deters crime. For instance, one study found that murders decreased by nearly one-third when the death penalty was reinstated in New York in 1995. Death penalty supporters cite this finding to support their argument that the existence of the death penalty deters criminals from committing murder. However, another study found that states without the death penalty have murder rates below the national average. This study is cited by opponents of capital punishment, who reject the claim that the death penalty deters murder. Students need context and clear, informed discussion if they are to think critically and make informed decisions.

The Hot Topics series is designed to help young people wade through the glut of fact, opinion, and rhetoric so that they can think critically about controversial issues. Only by reading and thinking critically will they be able to formulate a viewpoint that is not simply the parroted views of others. Each volume of the series focuses on one of today's most pressing social issues and provides a balanced overview of the topic. Carefully crafted narrative, fully documented primary and secondary source quotes, informative sidebars, and study questions all provide excellent starting points for research and discussion. Full-color photographs and charts enhance all volumes in the series. With its many useful features, the Hot Topics series is a valuable resource for young people struggling to understand the pressing issues of the modern era.

INTRODUCTION

A TROUBLING PROBLEM

Self-injury is a problem with many names; it has been called self-mutilation, self-inflicted violence, parasuicide, self-harm, or just "cutting." Self-injury means cutting, burning, hitting, scraping, or any sort of deliberate wounding of the skin and tissue in order to cope with serious psychological distress and overwhelming emotional pain.

Self-injury researchers and psychological and medical experts around the world are increasingly concerned about the apparent rise in the incidence of self-injury, especially in young people. It not only causes emotional problems but also can be physically dangerous when self-injurers "go too far" and, for instance, cut or burn too deeply, experience deep wound infections, or occasionally and accidentally inflict permanent damage, disability, or death. Society's awareness of the issue of self-injury and its dangers has made the behavior a topic of intense interest in some segments of the public. Teachers, parents, and other concerned people struggle to understand self-injury and figure out what to do about it. Myths and misunderstandings abound, while people who self-injure live with the secret shame of harming themselves yet are often convinced that they must self-injure to survive.

Some self-injurers just want to be left alone, and others desperately wish that they could stop, but all people who self-injure want to be respected and treated with compassion. Too often, others react judgmentally and with fear, horror, and disgust.

They may label the self-injurer as attention-seeking, manipulative, suicidal, or "crazy." None of these labels is accurate.

The American Self-Harm Information Clearing House is dedicated to educating everyone about self-harm and the important function it plays in meeting the needs of someone who does not know how to cope in any other way. The organization says, "The first step toward coping with self-injurious behavior is education: bringing reliable information about who self-injures, why they do it, and how they can learn to stop to people who self-injure and to their friends, loved ones, and medical caregivers."[1] However, the goal of widespread education is not without controversy in the medical and psychological community. The American Self-Harm Information Clearing House, for example, subscribes to the view that educating communities and school populations about the problem of self-injury will help to reduce the incidence of the disorder, while increasing compassion and outreach to those who self-harm. The organization subscribes to the theory that, for a variety of psychological, biological, and environmental reasons, individuals develop an overwhelming need to self-injure in order to relieve tension and stress.

Other experts worry that the causes of self-injury are not so clear-cut. Boys Town parenting experts Kimberly DeRuyck and Jennifer Resetar, for instance, cite peer pressure as one possible cause of self-injury. This theory is based on the idea that young people can learn self-injurious behavior from friends, Internet sites, or the media, imitate it, and even become attracted to trying the behavior because they have heard about it in educational programs. Sociologist Sarah Hodgson argues that the chances of people beginning to self-injure "increase as information on self-injury is becoming more widely available."[2] If this is true, some experts say, then general education and awareness about self-injury can be dangerous, especially in school populations where it can actually spread the behavior. No one is sure whether self-injury is always a symptom of an underlying psychological disorder or whether it can be a learned behavior. However, the controversy is an important one because the answer could determine what treatment or prevention approach is best.

Coping with self-injury requires learning about what it is and is not, understanding the reasons that it occurs, recognizing its dangers, and knowing how to meet the needs of self-injurers so that they can develop healthy ways to avoid the practice. Yet, the scientific and psychological knowledge about self-injury is still incomplete. Self-injurers, says counselor, writer, and advocate Deb Martinson, are individuals who

> come from all walks of life and all economic brackets. People who harm themselves may be male or female; gay, straight, or bi; Ph.D.s or high-school dropouts; rich or poor; and live in any country in the world. Some . . . manage to function effectively in demanding jobs; they are teachers, therapists, medical professionals, lawyers, professors, engineers. Some are on disability. Some are highly achieving high-school students. Their ages typically range from early teens to early 60s, although they may be older or younger.[3]

Many self-injurers want to be left alone and respected, but too often others react to them with fear, horror, and disgust.

Because self-injurers can be so different, researchers and therapists cannot offer simple answers about who they are, why they self-harm, or how to help them choose not to self-injure. Nevertheless, most experts agree that self-injury is an ultimately self-destructive activity and that it is an indication of underlying emotional issues that need to be resolved.

Self-injury can be overcome, depending on the willingness and readiness of each individual. Martinson advises self-injurers, "Deciding to stop self-injury is a very personal decision. You may have to consider it for a long time before you decide that you're ready to commit to a life without scars and bruises."[4] When that decision is made, time and effort are required to achieve recovery, but former self-injurers say the work is worth it. One anonymous young woman voices perhaps the most important benefit of understanding her self-injury and fighting to recover. She says, "In the most basic sense, I finally stopped when I learned how to love myself again."[5]

(Note: As you read, keep in mind that some material in this book may be triggering for some people; please keep yourself safe.)

HARMING ONESELF

Samantha, at age fourteen, feels bad about her body. When she compares herself to her "perfect" mother, she believes her looks and weight fall far short of the ideal. Her worry over how she looks makes her feel insecure about whether she is a worthwhile person, too. Samantha began making cuts on her forearms when she was twelve years old. She is able to hide the cuts and scars from others by wearing long-sleeved clothing, even in summer. She explains, "When things are going well for me, I do not cut myself, but when I start to feel worried about my body I want to punish myself for how I look."[6]

Jack, a seventeen-year-old eleventh grader cuts his arms, too. He feels overwhelmed by the stresses in his life and has trouble dealing with his anger and emotional hurt. He says, "Sometimes I feel numb, and inflicting pain is the only way I truly feel something."[7] Jack successfully hides his activity from others, as Samantha does, but Chrissie, a woman in her late twenties, cannot hide her injuries from the world. She first hurt herself in childhood by rubbing her skin with a pencil eraser until it bled. As an adult, however, she began using knives and razor blades to cut all over her body so deeply that she required emergency room visits and hundreds of stitches to close the wounds. Pam, a college student, burns herself with an iron and then pours water over the burns so that they will hurt more and not heal. Luke, a middle-aged man, has hurt himself in many ways; he has cut himself, burned himself, and poured acid on his hands. He does not have to force himself to stand the pain. He explains, "It's like a drug. Sometimes I don't realize I'm even doing it."[8]

Defining Self-Injury

Samantha, Jack, Pam, Chrissie, and Luke may be of different ages, use different tactics, experience different feelings, and explain their behaviors in different ways, but they all have one thing in common—they use self-injury to cope with their lives and emotions. Self-injury may also be called self-harm or self-mutilation. In their book *Self-Injury in Youth: The Essential Guide to Assessment and Intervention*, researchers Mary K. Nixon and Nancy L. Heath refer to it as "Nonsuicidal self-injury (NSSI)" and explain, "It can be defined as purposely inflicting injury that results in immediate tissue damage, done without suicidal intent and not socially sanctioned within one's culture nor for display. . . . NSSI includes, but is not limited to, cutting, pin-scratching, carving, burning, and self-hitting."[9]

The "nonsuicidal" part of Nixon's and Heath's definition is important. At one time, medical experts lumped self-injury together with suicide attempts and labeled them as "parasuicide"—near or resembling suicide. Today, however, most knowledgeable people reject that definition. Even people like Chrissie who injure themselves severely, say experts, are not trying to commit suicide nor are they making suicidal gestures. They do not self-injure because they want to die. They have an emotional problem or psychological disorder that causes them to attack their skin and the tissue beneath the skin in a way that causes injury, bleeding, wounds, or marks. But the attack is a coping mechanism and a way to relieve negative or unpleasant emotions, not an effort to disable or kill themselves.

A Secret Shame to Ease the Pain

Some experts, such as social worker Elana Premack Sandler, say that the goal of self-injury is not even to permanently change or scar the body, although scars are the usual outcome. Actually, self-injury is motivated by an attempt to deal with life rather than to escape life. In a strange way, it is an attempt to save oneself—to prevent the misery and depression that might lead to suicide—rather than an attempt to destroy oneself. For example, Sandler describes one teenage girl whose parents hospitalized

Some experts say that self-injurers are attempting to deal with their lives, not to escape them.

her when they discovered that she was cutting herself. In the hospital, the girl was prevented by staff members from cutting herself, and, then, she did attempt suicide. Sandler says, "I can't help but think about how that experience [the withdrawal of her coping tool] might have contributed to her suicide attempt."[10] Without the alternative of self-injury, the girl lapsed into hopelessness and wanted to die.

Medical doctors, psychologists, social workers, and other experts do not always agree about the definition of self-injury, but Sandler and most others emphatically differentiate the goals of self-injury from suicide attempts. In addition, Sandler and most others agree with Nixon and Heath in describing self-injury as a private activity, not a public one. Therefore, it is not a bid for attention. Unlike the skin "disfigurement" of tattoos or body piercings that are meant to be seen, the scars of self-injury are not displayed to the public. This means that most self-injurers try to hide the evidence of their self-harm. It means that they rarely cut or burn or harm themselves in the presence of other people. Psychologist Tracy Alderman explains,

> Most people who get tattooed and/or pierced are proud of their new decorations. They want to show others their ink, their studs, their plugs. They want to tell the story of the pain, the fear, the experience. In contrast, those who hurt themselves generally don't tell anyone about it. Self-injurers go to great lengths to cover and disguise their wounds and scars. Self-injurers are not proud of their new decorations."[11]

Laura, a twenty-one-year-old British woman describes how ashamed she was of the signs of her self-injury. Laura began cutting her arms and legs with razor blades when she was nineteen years old. Even though cutting relieved the tension she felt, she was terribly worried that people would find out what she was doing. She remembers,

> Later I always felt embarrassed about it. I used to do my utmost to try and hide it from others; if this meant wearing jumpers [sweaters] in the summer then that's what I did. I never wore a skirt that would reveal anything. It is only now, two years after I first cut myself that I actually feel comfortable wearing anything that may show some of my scars. The embarrassment was horrible as I felt completely alone and isolated.[12]

Is Repeated Self-Injury a Disorder?

Laura sometimes cut herself more than three times a day and, despite her sense of shame, continued this behavior daily for months at a time. Repeated episodes of cutting or attacking one's skin are key features of the definition of self-injury according to many experts. In 1993 psychiatrists Armando R. Favazza and Richard J. Rosenthal suggested that self-injurers should be diagnosed as having repetitive self-harm syndrome or repetitive self-mutilation syndrome. By their definition, a person who, for instance, injures himself or herself just once would not be diagnosed with the syndrome. But a person who repeats the behavior would be diagnosed with a psychological disorder. Some of the symptoms of the disorder include:

1. Preoccupation with harming oneself physically;
2. [Repeated] failure to resist impulses to harm oneself physically, resulting in the destruction or alteration of body tissue;
3. Increasing sense of tension immediately before the act of self-harm;
4. Gratification or a sense of relief when committing the act of self-harm;
5. The act of self-harm is not associated with conscious suicidal intent and is not in response to a delusion, hallucination . . . or serious mental retardation.[13]

Diagnosis of Self-Injury Today

Despite the recommendation of Favazza, Rosenthal, and others, clinicians (health professionals who work with and treat patients) still do not have a specific diagnosis for people who self-injure. Instead, clinicians typically diagnose people with the symptoms of self-injury as having other psychological or emotional disorders that lead them to self-harm. In the United States, clinicians use the standards and criteria set out by the American Psychiatric Association to diagnose psychological syndromes and problems. The symptoms of syndromes are described in a manual called the *Diagnostic and Statistical Manual of Mental Disorders, 4th Edition, Text Revision (DSM-IV-TR)*. Using the *DSM-IV-TR*, clinicians generally diagnose a person who self-injures as having one of the psychological disorders described in the manual. In this system, self-injury is just one symptom of another psychological disorder.

Self-Injury and Borderline Personality Disorder

One of the most common diagnoses for people who self-injure is called borderline personality disorder (BPD). The major characteristic of this disorder is "instability." People with BPD do not have stable relationships with other people. They do not have stable emotions, either, and may become very angry, panicky,

Jessicka Fodera

Singer and band member Jessicka Fodera no longer injures herself, but she has explained why she was drawn to the behavior in the past. She says,

The question might be why did I cut myself so much? I initially started cutting myself at an early age out of frustration. Cutting tends to relieve anger. Many self-injurers like myself have enormous amounts of rage within and are sometimes afraid to express it outwardly, we injure ourselves as a way of venting these feelings without hurting others. When intense feelings built, I became overwhelmed and unable to deal with it. By causing pain, I could reduce the level of emotional stress to a bearable one. As a teenager it was an escape from the numbness, many of those who self-injure say they do it in order to feel something, to know that they're still alive.

Quoted in Gabrielle, "Famous Self-injurers," Self-Injury. net. http://self-injury.net/media/famous-self-injurers.

or despairing when other people seem to "let them down" or not care enough about them. Borderline personality disorder often means acting on emotional impulse rather than thinking things through. It means having mood swings or intense emotions that can change quickly—for example, from being extremely happy to being terribly anxious or depressed. People with BPD also have a poor self-image; they report feeling empty and worthless. They are afraid of losing loved ones, fear being rejected or unloved, and may frantically try to prevent other people from abandoning them, sometimes for no good reason.

The *DSM-IV-TR* lists nine symptoms of BPD. It requires that a person must evidence at least five of the nine symptoms to be diagnosed with borderline personality disorder. The fifth symptom on the list is: "Recurrent suicidal behavior, gestures, or threats, or self-mutilating behavior."[14] By this criterion, self-injury is not much different than attempted suicide. It is one symptom of disordered behavior, along with feeling bad about

Borderline personality disorder can cause sudden mood swings, including going from extreme happiness to extreme depression and anxiety.

oneself, and experiencing impulsive despair. A person who self-injures and also shows symptoms of instability may be diagnosed with BPD.

Self-Injury and Mood Disorders

People who self-injure might be diagnosed as having mood disorders instead of BPD. Mood disorders include depression and bipolar disorder. Depression is characterized by constant sadness, lack of energy, feelings of hopelessness and worthlessness, and thoughts of suicide. It is believed to be caused by an imbalance of chemicals in the brain. Bipolar disorder is characterized by moods that swing between the extremes of depression and excited, energetic thoughts and feelings. It also is thought to be related to changes in the normal chemicals in the brain. Mood disorders are listed in *DSM-IV-TR* and diagnosed according to lists of symptoms. When a person who self-injures also reports depressions or extreme mood swings or suicidal thoughts, a clinician might diagnose a mood disorder. The depression is assumed to be causing the symptom of self-harm. However, self-injury is not listed as one of the symptoms of depression or bipolar disorder.

THEY WANT TO LIVE

"Typically, cutters say they don't want to die—they're cutting themselves to feel alive."—Denise Brandon, professor, University of Tennessee Extension Family and Consumer Sciences Department.

Quoted in Kristi Nelson, *Knoxville (TN) News Sentinel*, June 1, 2010. www.knoxnews.com/news/2010/jun/01/woman-draws-her-own-e.

Self-Injury as an Obsessive-Compulsive Disorder

Another psychological disorder associated with brain chemical imbalances is called obsessive-compulsive disorder (OCD). OCD is marked by repeated and long-lasting thoughts and worries that will not go away. It is also characterized by the need, or compulsion, to repeat certain activities, such as constant hand-washing, so as to ward off some terrible feeling or disaster; the compulsion may be so overwhelming that the person has little time to engage in normal activities. Sometimes, people with OCD may compulsively harm themselves. The self-injury usually takes the form of hair pulling (from the head, body, eyelashes, or eyebrows) or constant picking or scratching at the skin. If a person who self-injures does so compulsively rather than impulsively

People with OCD may compulsively harm themselves by pulling hair from the head, body, eyelashes, and eyebrows.

and feels that he or she must pull out hair or damage skin to prevent something terrible from happening, that person may be diagnosed with OCD.

Self-Injury, Anxiety, and Trauma

DSM-IV-TR also lists a large category of anxiety disorders, and sometimes people who self-injure are diagnosed with an anxiety disorder. Since people who self-injure may do so to relieve stress or to calm themselves, some clinicians believe that self-injury can arise from serious, prolonged anxiety and tension. The self-injury is a symptom of the anxiety disorder and is used to decrease anxiousness, tension, and overwhelming feelings of panic and worry.

Many experts who study or treat self-injury see the disorder—at least sometimes—as a symptom of post-traumatic stress disorder (PTSD). This diagnosis suggests that the cause of self-injury is a trauma that the person has undergone in the past. A trauma is any sudden, overwhelming event that leaves a person feeling powerless, helpless, or in danger. Some examples of traumas include living through a severe earthquake, becoming a prisoner of war, being raped or assaulted, or being physically abused as a child. These experiences can be so emotionally upsetting that they are difficult to accept or adjust to, even when the traumatic events are over. Some scientists suggest that the trauma may even affect the brain by causing a chemical imbalance. People with PTSD may have a range of symptoms that include fear, trouble sleeping, stress, anxiety, anger, abusing drugs or alcohol to numb their feelings, and depression. People who self-injure may be diagnosed with PTSD if they are coping with their trauma by hurting themselves to deal with and soothe their feelings.

Unsatisfactory Diagnoses

According to diagnostic standards today, people may self-injure as a result of several different psychological disorders. Self-injury is not a diagnosis and often cannot even be diagnosed unless the self-injurer tells a clinician about the problem. As a secretive behavior, it can go undiagnosed for years. This situation is disturbing to many self-injury researchers and clinicians. They want to agree on a better definition of self-injury, educate the public and professionals about the importance of identifying and helping self-injurers, and diagnose self-injury as a disorder in and of itself. Many experts also argue that people who self-injure do not necessarily suffer from some other disorder.

According to the mental health advocacy organization National Alliance on Mental Illness, 75 percent of people who are diagnosed with borderline personality disorder self-injure. However, some experts wonder if these people truly have BPD or if they are merely diagnosed with BPD because they injure themselves. In 1997, for instance, psychologist S. Herpertz and his colleagues studied people who self-injure and discovered that only 48 percent of them met the criteria for having

Self-injury is usually difficult to diagnose because self-injurers are very secretive about their habit.

borderline personality disorder. When the scientists excluded the symptom of self-injury, they reported that only 28 percent of self-injurers met the other criteria for BPD. Some scientists have argued that too many clinicians simply diagnose BPD whenever they discover that a person self-injures.

New Diagnosis Needed

Other clinicians reject the BPD diagnosis and instead choose another disorder from the *DSM-IV-TR* called impulse-control disorder. This disorder is used as a diagnosis for anyone who has strong impulses or temptations that are hard to resist. The person diagnosed with this disorder feels great tension when trying to resist the temptation and then experiences relief after giving in to it. Today, many scientists and clinicians argue that self-injury should be a diagnosis on its own, perhaps defined as a type of impulse disorder. In 2010 the American Psychiatric Association was in the process of revising its manual and preparing the *DSM-V* for publication. A proposed change for the *DSM-V* is to include a diagnosis called nonsuicidal self injury (NSSI). The diagnosis would include criteria such as intentionally self-harming at least five times in the last year in a way that is not trivial or common (e.g., biting one's nails is common) and harming oneself without suicidal intent. It also proposes that the person must have at least two of the following four symptoms:

1. Negative feelings or thoughts, such as depression, anxiety, tension, anger, generalized distress, or self-criticism, occurring in the period immediately prior to the self-injurious act.
2. Prior to engaging in the act, a period of preoccupation with the intended behavior that is difficult to resist.
3. The urge to engage in self-injury occurs frequently, although it might not be acted upon.
4. The activity is engaged in with a purpose; this might be relief from a negative feeling/cognitive [thinking] state or interpersonal difficulty or induction of [leading to] a positive feeling state. The patient anticipates these will occur either during or immediately following the self-injury.[15]

Members of the American Psychiatric Association have spent years discussing and analyzing changes for the new diagnostic manual. They expect to complete the *DSM-V* and release the updated manual in 2013. At that time, clinicians and other professionals hope to have an NSSI diagnosis that includes criteria that define self-injury in an accurate, standardized way. Ideally, the diagnosis will also help clinicians to better understand self-injury and to help the people who are diagnosed with the disorder.

PHYSICAL EXPRESSIONS OF PAIN

"Some turn to alcohol, narcotics, or other destructive substances. Others binge, purge, or starve themselves. For more and more people, however, comfort comes from razor blades, knives, scissors, and other household implements that they use to carve physical expressions of their anguish on their skin."—Karen Conterio and Wendy Lader, cofounders of S.A.F.E. Alternatives.

Karen Conterio and Wendy Lader, *Bodily Harm*. New York: Hyperion, 1998, p. 16.

Who Self-Injures?

Accurate diagnosis and understanding of self-injury is important to medical and psychological professionals today because self-injury seems to be a growing problem around the world. In 2010, in the *Journal of the American Board of Family Medicine*, psychologist Patrick Kerr and his team reported "an increasing prevalence of self-injury, especially among adolescents [teens] and young adults."[16] No one knows why self-injury might be increasing, but the scientific team says that existing information suggests that approximately 15 percent of teens admit to some form of self-injury. In the United States, approximately 1 to 4 percent of adults self-injure. Among college students, the rate of self-injury is reported to be between 17 to 35 percent. Self-injury seems to begin in youth. Most people start to self-injure between the ages of thirteen and fifteen. Experts used to believe that girls and women were much more likely to self-injure than boys and men, but Kerr and

Self-Injury in Prison

The incidence of self-injury in prison populations is known to be quite high. A survey of prisoners in the United Kingdom found that approximately 30 percent of female prisoners and 6 percent of male prisoners injured themselves. The younger the inmates were, the more likely they were to experiment with self-injury.

In the United States, approximately 2 to 4 percent of all inmates are known to self-injure. Prisoners most often cut themselves with sharp objects, swallow dangerous objects, bang their heads against walls, or open old wounds. According to Lorry Schoenly, a correctional system nurse, prison staff usually believe that prisoners self-injure out of boredom or to get attention. She says, however, that the self-injury is "motivated by a 'coping deficit' when dealing with feelings of depression or powerlessness." In prison, people are indeed powerless, and they often suffer with psychological disorders. Researchers in the UK report that 70 percent of prison inmates have two or more mental disorders. In the United States, a 2009 Harvard study reported that about 25 percent of inmates in jails and prisons suffer with serious mental illnesses such as schizophrenia, bipolar disorder, or depression. People in prison have little independence and often are allowed few supportive social contacts. Experts theorize that both the prison environment and previous psychological disorders play a role in increasing the risk of self-injury among prisoners.

Lorry Schoenly, "I'm Gonna Hurt Myself," Correctional Nurse.net, February 8, 2010. http://lorryschoenly. wordpress.com/tag/self-injury-behavior.

Prison can aggravate the tendency to engage in self-injury.

his team say that current research shows that males and females are equally likely to self-injure. Males are more likely to burn and hit themselves; females are more likely to burn or cut themselves.

In other parts of the world, young people seem especially vulnerable to self-injury also. According to the British National Self Harm Network, the United Kingdom has one of the worst problems with self-injury throughout Europe. The rate is estimated to be four hundred out of every one hundred thousand people. In 2008 child psychologist Nicola Madge conducted a study of teens in seven different European countries that showed that three in ten girls and one in ten boys had either harmed themselves or thought of harming themselves during the past year. In this study, cutting was the most common form of self-injury, and about 25 percent of the young people interviewed had successfully hidden their self-injury from everyone. Madge concluded that statistics about self-injury probably do not reveal the extent of the disorder among European youth. She says, "This research shows that self-harm is an international, widespread yet often hidden problem."[17] In Canada, one 2008 study found that 16.9 percent of teens had harmed themselves, and in Australia, one out of every sixteen young people has engaged in self-injury.

Statistics and information about self-injury are not available in many parts of the world, but most experts believe that the disorder is common everywhere, although different methods of harm may be used in different places. In Pakistan, for example, self-poisoning is often preferred and can result in death, even though suicide is not the person's intention. Experts say that self-injurers who survive are not reported to medical professionals because such self-harm is against the law in Pakistan and is considered a sin in the Muslim religion. British physician and poisons expert Michael Eddleston calls self-harm "an overlooked tragedy in the developing world."[18] In Sri Lanka, for instance, poison is also a common means of self-harm, and, as a result, Sri Lanka, Eddleston says, has a very high suicide rate (40 per 100,000 people per year) compared with the British suicide rate (8 per 100,000 people). Eddleston explains that most of the young people who die of suicide from self-poisoning do not mean to kill themselves. They are trying to cope with stress or difficult problems by means of self-injury and die accidentally.

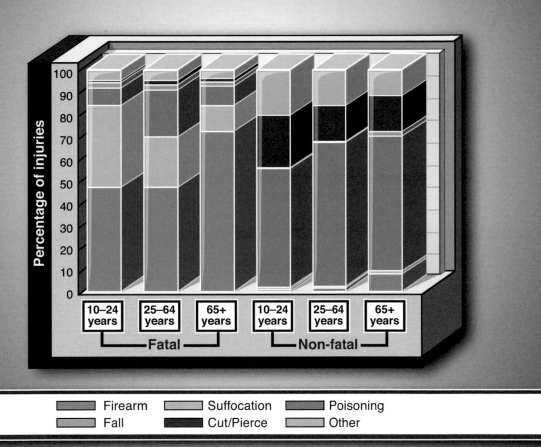

Percentage of Self-Harm Injuries, by Age Group, Disposition, and Mechanism, United States, 2002–2006

Percentage of injuries

100 90 80 70 60 50 40 30 20 10 0

| 10–24 years | 25–64 years | 65+ years | 10–24 years | 25–64 years | 65+ years |

Fatal — Non-fatal

Firearm Suffocation Poisoning
Fall Cut/Pierce Other

Trying to Understand Self-Injury

The goal of nonsuicidal self-injury may not be death or permanent disability, yet that is a real risk run by people who repeatedly self-injure, no matter what the method. Self-injury is dangerous, and it can be hard to understand as a method of coping. Why do people cut or burn or poison themselves? Just as experts try to accurately define and diagnose self-injury, they also try to identify the causes of self-injury and explain how some people develop the strong need to hurt themselves.

CHAPTER 2

THE CAUSES OF
SELF-INJURY

Repetitive, nonsuicidal self-injury is a coping tool, but how and why people choose it as a way to deal with negative thoughts and feelings is a big question. Both experts and people who self-injure suggest several different theories about its causes and agree that people self-harm for a variety of reasons. Although professionals acknowledge that the causes of self-injury are still not well understood, almost everyone agrees that self-injury is a method of dealing with intense feelings and extreme emotional pain.

Emotional Pain

Sarah Michelle Fisher has struggled with self-injury and explains the emotions that can cause people to harm themselves in this way:

> Have you ever felt so aggressive, afraid, angry, belittled, betrayed, bitter, cheated, confused, depressed, deceived, disappointed, foolish, empty, insecure, hopeless, frustrated, lonely, lost, miserable, numb, pained, picked-on, rejected, small, sorry, stupid, suffocated, tense, terrified, useless, un-wanted, un-loved, un-important, worried, wrung-out, worn-out, withdrawn, ticked, tortured, trapped, and blank that you've turned to hurting yourself just to feel something different?[19]

The emotions that Fisher lists can all be overwhelming and painful, and self-injury can indeed change those feelings or allow self-injurers to express them, at least temporarily. Self-injury treatment experts Karen Conterio, an alcohol and addictions counselor, and Wendy Lader, a clinical psychologist, say that the purposes behind self-injury can be divided into two major categories. The first is "analgesic or palliative," meaning eliminating or reducing pain. The second is "communicative."[20] By Conterio and Lader's definition, this means expressing and acting out emotional pain either to oneself or to others in a cry for help. Conterio and Lader quote Susan L. as an example of the analgesia self-injury can bring about. Susan says,

> Before I self-injure, I fantasize about the relief I'll get. I see myself making deep cuts and producing lots of blood. The blood is so soothing. It's warm. While I do it, I go very fast. I feel very much in control. I decide when to stop.

> During the cutting, I feel calm. I feel powerful, and I feel focused. After self-injury, I feel so much relief. I feel very calm. My inside pain and feelings are gone. I go to the emergency room and can't even tell the doctor why I did it because the feelings are so buried.[21]

Self-injury can be analgesic, palliative, or a way of crying out for help.

Susan L. uses her self-injury to feel better about herself; it is a soothing action for her. Other self-injurers may be communicating how worthless they are or that they deserve to be punished. Conterio and Lader describe Jared T. who calls his self-injury "the tangible face to my intangible pain—see my pain!" Jared thinks, "I'll show them just how worthless I am, and how much I hurt."[22] Other self-injurers may believe that bleeding from injuries cleanses them of the emotional poison inside them or is a

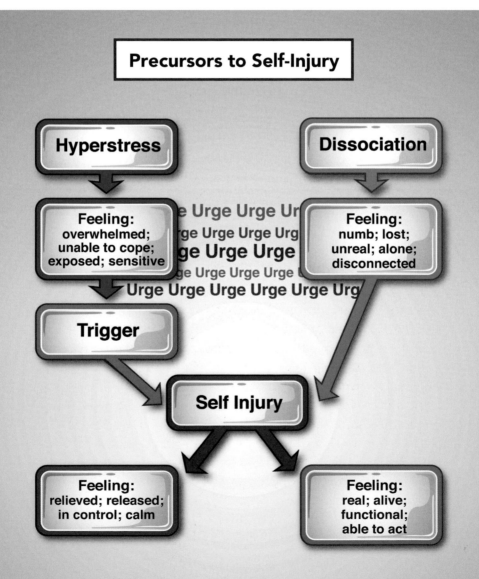

way to punish themselves for their sins. However, Conterio and Lader explain that self-injurers cannot usually describe what about them is so sinful or bad. Even when self-injurers keep their actions hidden, they may be secretly wishing that someone would see their pain and care enough to want to save them from the injuries and reassure them that they are good and worthwhile. But most of the time, explain Contario, Lader, and other experts in the self-harm field, such rescue is not possible. Self-injurers feel so helpless, worthless, and ashamed of who they are that they cannot believe the good things others say about them.

HURTING TO FEEL

"It's like when you hold your breath, hold your breath. You just feel you are going to blow up. Self-harm is like when you breathe again."—Tor, twenty-four-year-old British woman and former self-injurer.

Quoted in "Self-Harming Since the Age of Fifteen," BBC News, December 18, 2007. http://news.bbc.co.uk/2/hi/health/7142128.stm.

Trauma During Childhood

How can people come to feel so bad about themselves that they need to hurt and injure themselves? One theory proposed by self-injury researchers and clinicians is abuse and/or trauma during childhood. Conterio says that in surveys, about half of all people who self-injure report being abused as children. Armando Favazza, who wrote the first professional book on self-harm, also said that childhood abuse is commonly linked with self-injury and eating disorders (another way of harming oneself). Clinicians who treat self-injurers report the same connection with early abuse. Childhood abuse can cause a psychological problem called dissociation, a kind of psychological defense against extreme trauma in which people disconnect from their emotions and experiences. They "zone out" to protect themselves and are numb to emotional or physical pain. They feel as if the trauma is happening to someone else or as if they are removed from their bodies. Dissociation is a survival tool, but when abused people grow up, they may experience dissociation habitually and uncontrollably. They may then injure themselves so as to feel something or "feel alive" again. Other people who were abused may use self-injury for the opposite effect—to make overpoweringly painful feelings and memories stop.

People who self-injure often remember terrible childhoods that may be one reason that they hurt themselves. Susan L., for example, was beaten by her mother and constantly called names and told that she was worthless and stupid. A neighbor raped her repeatedly, but her mother did not believe Susan when she tried to talk about the abuse. Susan's father did not help her and ignored the trauma she was suffering.

Liz C. was treated cruelly by her parents, too. Her mentally ill mother beat her regularly and once tried to kill her. Her father sexually abused her throughout her childhood. Both parents were very strict. They did not allow Liz to go to dances or to movies with friends. Liz was never allowed to display any anger or talk about her feelings. She says her parents were "religious fanatics" who made her believe that any happiness was a sin. Like Susan, Liz began hurting herself in childhood. She cut her arms, scratched and bit herself, burned her skin with cigarettes, and stabbed herself with pencils. Liz remembers the first time she hurt herself at age thirteen, after a clash with her mother. She recalls, "You didn't get angry with Mom, because if you did, you would get hurt. I don't know why the idea came across my head—I'm not sure if I was trying to kill myself—but I ended up self-injuring, and I got an immediate release."[23]

Conterio and Lader say that it is easy to understand why abused children grow up to self-injure. They are filled with anger and rage about the cruel treatment, but they cannot hurt the people who are cruel to them. They cannot even release the anger in words. Instead of hurting the abuser, they release the rage by hurting themselves. Since such children often grow up believing that they are worthless and deserve to be cruelly treated, many hurt themselves to express self-hate. Often, they feel shame about the abuse and believe that it was their fault. Other

Childhood abuse is commonly associated with self-injury.

self-injurers try to gain control of their bodies through the damage they do. Their bodies were not cared for by their parents. Instead, their bodies were treated like objects that could be used.

Sometimes, self-injury is a way of reenacting the abuse or trauma. Over and over, by hurting his or her body the self-injurer relives the previous damage done. And when self-injurers harm themselves, at least they are in control of the injury. It is their decision and a way of saying that they are not victims anymore. They can decide what is going to happen and when it will stop.

In a strange way, self-injury can even be an emotional way to hurt the abuser. One self-injurer told the therapist who was helping her that she had to cut herself as a way to hurt her mother. She said, "Can't you see? I had to cut her loose!"[24] Conterio and Lader explain that without the loving bond and care between parent and child, abused people cannot feel good about themselves and cannot learn to express their negative feelings in a healthy way. They often cannot even allow themselves to recognize the angry or sad feelings that they experience. Instead, they physically attack themselves, and as time passes they come to depend upon self-injury as a way to survive.

TOO MANY MYTHS

"I wanted to try to dispel some myths and misconceptions: that self-injury constitutes a suicidal gesture; that self-injurers are by definition severely emotionally disturbed; that they are necessarily the product of terrible, abusive environments."—Caroline Kettlewell, author and former self-injurer.

Caroline Kettlewell.com. www.carolinekettlewell.com/books/skin_game/synopsis.html.

Unloved and Uncared For

At least half of all self-injurers, according to clinicians such as Favazza and Conterio and surveys of self-injurers, have never been physically or sexually abused, but psychiatrists Digby Tantam and Nick Huband explain that physical or sexual abuse is not necessary to explain self-injury. People who did not experience warmth and approval from their families may suffer from a kind of emotional abuse. They may grow up feeling neglected or unloved. They may have had strict parents who demanded "perfect" behavior and did not allow their children the freedom to be themselves, express their emotions, or make decisions. The parents may have been cold and controlling or judgmental and critical. They may have treated their children's emotions as trivial or punished them for revealing negative emotions or denied that their children's feelings were real. This is called invalidating, and some self-injury researchers say that self-injurers grew up in "invalidating environments."[25] Abuse is one way to invalidate someone, but it may be physical, sexual, or emotional.

The two emotional themes that may trigger self-injury are powerlessness and loneliness.

Tantam and Huband say, "Studies find that there are limited ranges of emotional themes that are likely to trigger self-injury. In our own research, the two that were far and away the most frequent were feeling powerless and feeling uncared for."[26] It is easy to understand that abused children would grow up feeling powerless and uncared for. But not all research supports the idea that abuse triggers self-injury.

In 2008 psychologists E. David Klonsky and Anne Moyer studied the relationship between self-injury and sexual abuse. They concluded that childhood sexual abuse was no more common in people who self-injure than in the rest of the population. They did think that severe and prolonged sexual abuse might be a cause of self-injury, but they were unable to prove it in their study. In 2006 eighty-six female teens were studied by Lisa H. Glassman and her research team at Harvard, and that study yielded different results. The researchers did not find a relationship between physical abuse and self-injury, but they did find that sexual abuse and emotional abuse were related to self-injury.

Releasing the "Safety Catch"

Physical, sexual, and emotional abuse may explain why many people resort to self-injury, but much more research is needed to really understand all of its environmental causes. Since many people are abused and do not become self-injurers, some researchers try to explore human psychology to explain why only some people who have experienced unloving or invalidating environments go on to develop a problem with self-injury. Tantam and Huband suggest that people have a "safety catch,"[27] or neurological response, that protects them from self-injury most of the time. The safety catch is the brain's way of protecting the body. People resist putting themselves in danger of injury and feel repugnance and shock when they see or even imagine such injuries because of their safety catch. However, the safety catch can be turned off or weakened if the type of self-injury is familiar or culturally acceptable. For example, piercing one's ears or undergoing surgery are familiar and acceptable in society. So the safety catch that protects people from harm is weakened in these situations. For most people, however, the idea of slashing

Social Exceptions to the Safety Catch

Digby Tantam and Nick Huband note many instances in which societies encourage people to release their self-injury safety catches. They explain that self-injury is or has been approved in almost every culture in the world. In Germany during the nineteenth century, for example, a scar on the face from a sword injury was honorable, so young men would cut each other with sabers to have a fashionable scar. Members of one sect of Islam beat themselves with chains, just as early Christians beat themselves during the Middle Ages, to bleed and atone for their sins. Almost everywhere in the world, people decorate themselves with tattoos and piercings of ears, noses, lips, navels, or other body parts. Modern people routinely undergo plastic surgeries for cosmetic purposes. Among the Padaung hill tribe in Thailand, women are made beautiful by wearing more and more brass rings around their necks until their necks are so stretched and elongated that they are known as "giraffe women." For other indigenous peoples around the world, scars and marks are used to decorate the body. People do not often consider such behaviors to be self-injury, but Tantam and Huband say they are. "Most people," they explain, "Go along with what is customary in their own culture."

Digby Tantam and Nick Huband, "The Psychological and Cultural Place of Self-Injury," in *Understanding Repeated Self-Injury*. New York: Palgrave Macmillan, 2009.

A Maori from New Zealand sports his tattoos. Some argue that tattooing is also a form of self-injury. Many cultures throughout history have used self-injury in rituals.

an arm with a razor blade on purpose is socially unacceptable, shocking, and repulsive because of the safety catch.

Tantam and Huband say that self-injurers are able to overcome or bypass their safety catch even though their actions are not familiar or accepted by society. Repeating self-injury actions is one way to overcome the safety catch. The individual gets more and more used to the sight and feeling of the injury and no longer is repulsed or shocked by the experience. Another way to overcome the safety catch is through social familiarity and cultural acceptance, such as, for instance, the bloodletting that is done in some tribes in New Guinea to initiate boys into manhood or the self-whipping that used to be practiced by some Christian groups in Europe. Psychiatrists and psychologists have also reported extreme self-injury in some severely mentally ill people and in children born with certain serious brain disorders, and in these cases, they suggest that the normal safety catch may be neurologically disrupted or turned off.

Born Vulnerable

Some researchers wonder whether the vulnerability to self-injury lies in the genes. Genes are the units of heredity in all living things. Most genes in humans are the same for everyone, but variations and changes in certain genes can determine whether a person is at risk for developing some problems or illnesses or is vulnerable to certain experiences in the environment. Scientists think that a variation in a gene or genes could possibly predispose some individuals to developing a self-injury disorder when the environment "pulls the trigger." A trigger for self-harm, for example, might be sexual abuse during childhood. An individual with certain gene variations might become a self-injurer when exposed to sexual abuse.

So far, the theory that a genetic vulnerability causes some to self-harm has yet to be proven as fact, but a recent study suggests that researchers may be on the right track. In 2010 veterinary researchers reported discovering a gene in Doberman pinscher dogs that was linked with compulsive behavior. The dogs with the gene variation exhibited compulsive behavior such as licking themselves until they caused open wounds

Scientists have discovered a gene in Doberman pinschers that is linked to compulsive behavior.

on their bodies. The veterinarians reported that the dogs developed this behavior in response to anxiety or stress. Nicholas Dodman, the leader of the research team, says that people with obsessive-compulsive disorder who injure themselves may have a similar gene variation. Other researchers now are trying to find out whether people with OCD might have a similar genetic predisposition. If they do, the gene or genes would not exactly cause the kind of self-injury sometimes seen with obsessive-compulsive disorder. But the genetic variation might explain why some people, when exposed to negative environmental triggers, would develop self-harm behaviors.

Harvard psychologist Matthew K. Nock also believes that gene variations could make people vulnerable to psychological disorders if they are exposed to environmental triggers and stress. He suggests that gene variations may make people more impulsive, more emotionally reactive, and less able to cope with stress. In an abusive or negative environment, such people may become anxious, depressed, and self-destructive. They may develop drug abuse problems, eating disorders, suicidal thoughts, and self-injury disorders. Many people who self-injure also have eating disorders, substance abuse problems, and psychological disorders such as depression and anxiety. Many also attempt or think about suicide. Nock suggests that all of these problems are just different forms of self-destructive behaviors, caused by the interaction between genes and life experiences. However, he warns that the true causes of self-injury are complex and that scientists are just beginning to understand how gene vulnerabilities and environmental triggers interact to cause psychological disorders. He explains that the idea of "'a gene for' behaviors such as self-injury is unrealistic and inaccurate."[28]

Made Vulnerable by Abuse

Genes are not the only cause of people developing brain variations and vulnerabilities. Some researchers have discovered that physical, emotional, or sexual abuse and mistreatment in early childhood can actually change the way that brains function. In both animals and people, scientists have discovered that early trauma can physically change the function of cells that are involved with the brain chemicals called dopamine and serotonin. These brain cells become "supersensitive" to dopamine, and studies suggest that sensitivity to dopamine can cause impulsive behavior and anxiety. It may also reduce sensitivity to pain. Decreased levels of serotonin in the brain have been shown in studies to be linked to impulsive behaviors, depression, and sui-cidal thoughts. Researchers are not sure of exactly how trauma in early childhood changes the brain's responses, but they theo-rize that the stress hormones released by the body in response to trauma trigger certain genes to turn on and react to the chemi-cals. These genes then "tell" the brain to develop and respond in a different way, and the brain becomes highly sensitive to stress. So changes to the brain from early childhood trauma may play a role in the development of self-injury disorders and the weaken-ing of the safety catch.

Self-Injury and Addiction

When the safety catch is overcome, for whatever reason, repeat-ed acts of self-injury become easier, and people may develop a kind of addiction to the behavior. Many people who self-injure feel little or no pain, even when their wounds are deep or seri-ous. This happens because the brain releases chemicals called endorphins whenever it receives pain signals from an injury. Tracy Alderman explains that endorphins act almost like mor-phine to reduce the amount of pain people feel. They are the body's way of reducing the stress that pain causes. She says, "Sometimes people who intentionally hurt themselves will even say that they felt a 'rush' or 'high' from the act. Given the role of endorphins, this makes perfect sense."[29]

Psychologist V.J. Turner argues that self-injury becomes habit-forming and addictive in the same way that some drugs become addictive. She says that the chemicals released by the brain in response to self-injury can "hook" people just as drugs like heroin and morphine do. She explains that being vulner-able to addiction may be rooted in traumatic childhood expe-riences, psychological or personality disorders, or being born with a vulnerability, or predisposition, to becoming addicted to substances or behaviors.

Many people who self-injure agree with Turner that self-injury is addictive. In an article for a website devoted to col-lecting information about self-injury, Justin Mills describes his former self-injury as an addiction that was almost religious. He writes, "Junkies live and die by their needle. I lived by my blade.

There is little [difference] between the two instruments: both penetrate the flesh causing extreme feelings of euphoria [extreme happiness]. Yet whereas the needle implants, the blade releases. All drugs and intoxicants constitute forms of self-destruction, or mutilation." Mills has recovered from his self-injury addiction, but he remembers cutting his legs with a razor blade every day for three years. When he was not cutting, he describes himself as feeling angry, depressed, helpless, and desperate. Cutting was like a drug for him that let him escape his terrible emotions. He says now he knows that, "one must be in a certain hopeless state of mind in order to feel the effects of the drug."[30]

Self-Injury as a Learned Behavior

While some researchers suggest that self-injury is a disease like cancer or diabetes, Turner argues that it is learned. First the self-injurer must experiment with harming him- or herself. Then, as he or she learns about the feeling of release or the soothing "benefits" or the "high," the action slowly becomes addictive. The urge to self-injure grows stronger and becomes more difficult to resist, even when the individual wants to stop. Self-injury becomes the drug that numbs emotional pain. As time passes, the self-injurer requires deeper and deeper damage to get the medicating effects, just like drug addicts need more and more drugs to get high.

Indeed, Mills first got the idea of cutting himself from a girlfriend. She self-injured by cutting her legs. One day, when he was feeling extremely angry and did not know how to get rid of the feeling, he impulsively tried cutting his own leg. Gradually, over time, the cutting habit became more severe and more frequent.

Many self-injury experts believe that the habit of injuring oneself may begin by imitation or example. Justin imitated his girlfriend, and some researchers have reported that other self-injurers first learned of the behavior from friends at school. In one 2010 study of middle and high schoolers, researchers Janis Whitlock and Amanda. Purington of Cornell University found groups of teens self-injuring together as a kind of sign of group membership.

Animals and Self-Injury

Experimental psychologists have reported self-injurious behavior in many animals, such as monkeys, lions, hyenas, rats, birds, dogs, and cats. The animals may lick themselves until sores develop, bite themselves, or tear at the skin with their claws. Researchers say that social isolation is a major reason for the behavior in captive animals. In small zoo or laboratory cages, animals are "prisoners," often isolated and separated from others of their kind.

Frustration is another cause of animal self-injury. For example, a captive animal may redirect its aggression from the human it cannot attack to its own body. It may be frustrated by an inability to reach food that it can see and, therefore, direct its aggression toward its body. A captive or domestic animal may be so frustrated by boredom or lack of stimulation that it compulsively licks or scratches itself or pulls out feathers or fur.

Some psychologists say that animal self-injury is very similar to self-injury in people. It is the result of anxiety in stressful situations in which the animal is powerless and has no control. The animals' self-injury becomes a way of coping, a way to reduce extreme stress.

In small zoos and laboratory cages, animals often feel isolated and tend to bite and lick themselves or tear at their skin with their claws.

Some researchers wonder whether self-injury might be contagious. In prisons, in psychiatric treatment hospitals, and in other residential settings, self-injury behaviors seem to spread among the populations like a sickness. In middle schools and high schools, teachers and counselors have reported epidemics of self-injury that seem to spread among students. However, in 1989 Favazza and Conterio reported that 91 percent of 240 female self-injurers in a research study had not known anyone who self-injured nor even heard of the behavior before they experimented with it or accidentally discovered it. Whitlock surveyed 2,875 college students in 2006 and discovered that more than one-third of those who self-injured had kept the behavior a secret from everyone. Studies such as these suggest that imitation of others is often not a factor in self-harm. Nevertheless, on the basis of other studies in 2006 and 2009, the Cornell research team that includes Whitlock, Purington, and others says about some self-injurers, "Our research suggests that the Internet and the increasing prevalence of self-injury in popular media, such as movies, books, and news reports . . . may play a role in the spread of self-injury."[31]

Whitlock explains that self-injury may be spread through a school or any social group because learning about instances of self-injury makes it seem socially acceptable and helps to weaken the safety catch against self-injury for other individuals. In a residential group, such as a prison or hospital, it is relatively easy to hear about or see the evidence of self-injury. In the larger society, modern use of the Internet can also make it simple to learn about instances of self-injury.

Whitlock says that in the anonymity of the Internet, young people can connect with others who self-injure and come to think of the behavior as normal and acceptable. They may be encouraged and supported in experimenting with self-injury. However, Whitlock believes the encouragement to self-injure increases or starts the behavior only in vulnerable people. A happy, well-adjusted teen, for example, would not become addicted to self-injury because of discovering a website where people discuss harming themselves. Contagion—or "catching" the sickness through contact and discussions with other self-injurers—would occur only among teens who do not know how to cope with their negative emotions and have "a low sense of self-worth."[32]

More Knowledge Needed

Research into the biological, environmental, and psychological causes of self-injury is just beginning, and scientists do not fully understand all the causes. Nock calls self-injury both "perplexing" and "harmful" and says that many important questions remain unanswered. He says of the research so far:

> Although impressive gains have been made, there is still much to learn about why people intentionally and repeatedly harm themselves. Future research on self-injury will not only advance the understanding, assessment, and treatment of this behavior problem, but will also improve the understanding of self-harm more broadly and of how to decrease such behaviors in order to help people live healthier and more adaptive lives.[33]

THE RISKS OF SELF-INJURY

Sometimes people argue that their self-injury is not a risky or negative action but a positive one—self-preserving and no different than any other coping tool. Karen Conterio and Wendy Lader say that these arguments include:

> "Self-injury doesn't hurt anyone."
> "Giving up self-injury will only make me hurt more."
> "If I don't self-injure, I'll end up killing myself."
> "It's my body and I can do whatever I want."
> "No one knows that I injure anyway."
> "I don't understand why it upsets others."[34]

Most professionals and experts, however, see self-injury as self-destructive. As time goes on, most self-injurers come to agree. Self-injury is not a positive way to deal with life. The risks of the behavior are physical, emotional, and social, and repetitive self-injurers do not learn healthy ways to cope with stress and pain.

Physical Risk and Major Self-Injury

Self-injury researcher Barent W. Walsh says that most self-injury carries little risk of permanent disability or death. He calls this common type of self-injury "low-lethality." But a nontypical kind of self-injury, called major self-injury, can result in real medical danger. It is called "medium-lethality" or "high-lethality,"[35] depending on the severity of the injury. Major self-injury includes such behaviors as breaking one's bones, amputating one's own limbs, severely cutting the genitals, or removing an eye from its socket. In the Western world, acts of major self-injury are usually committed by people who are seriously mentally ill. This kind of self-injury is true mutilation and can lead to permanent harm and death.

In other parts of the world, major self-injury may not be a result of mental illness but an extreme cry for help or an expression of hopeless, helpless despair. In Afghanistan, for example, major self-injury is prevalent among women. Afghan women have few rights and are often badly mistreated. They are beaten and abused by their husbands or in-laws, are often forced into arranged marriages at young ages, and receive little support or help from the government or society. Sometimes, these desperate women resort to pouring fuel on their bodies and

Some Afghan women immolate themselves to send a message to their abusers, usually their family.

setting themselves on fire. This practice is also referred to as self-immolation. In many of these cases, the women are choosing suicide to escape terrible situations, but at other times, the women are self-injuring in a very dangerous way in order to demonstrate their misery and stop their ongoing physical and emotional pain.

In 2008 filmmaker Olga Sadat went to Afghanistan to interview women in hospitals who had set themselves on fire. As she gained their trust, several of the women told Sadat about the circumstances that led to their self-injuries. Sadat reports that their aim was not suicide. The women hoped that they would be rescued. They wanted the people who were abusing them to understand how much they were suffering. They hoped these family members would stop them and show that they were valued. Often, the family members did nothing until it was too late. Sadly, this kind of major self-injury is usually fatal in a country where advanced medical treatment for severe burns is not available. Of the women Sadat interviewed, only one lived. Across the country, 70 percent of women who set fire to themselves die of their injuries.

Physical Risks and Common Self-Injury

Common self-injury in the industrialized world rarely carries the risk of death, but it does carry other medical risks, especially when self-injury is repetitive and impulsive. In his book *Treating Self-Injury* Walsh describes one of his patients, sixteen-year-old Sula. Sula had been cutting her arms and legs for three years, but one day the cuts were not enough to sooth and calm her. She became so upset that she impulsively snatched up a needle and pierced both her nipples. She was able to keep this injury secret until the wound in one nipple became infected, requiring medical treatment.

Infections are one common danger of self-injury. The British magazine for nurses, *Nursing Times*, warns, "People who injure themselves risk infections if their wounds are not treated properly. Cuts can become infected if a person uses non-sterile or dirty cutting instruments. It is also important not to share cutting implements with other people as many diseases, including

HIV and AIDS, can be caught this way. They are also at risk of permanent scarring from the cuts and wounds."[36]

Wounds from cutting can also be so deep or bleed so much that medical treatment is necessary. According to experts, about one in five self-injurers accidentally makes a life-threatening injury. Jennifer anonymously posted on the Internet her story of a mistaken life-threatening injury. She titled it "My Trip to the E.R." Jennifer was a high school student who lived with her grandparents and was already seeing a counselor to try to overcome her need to self-injure. One night, however, the urge to cut herself was very strong. She used a razor blade on her arm, but somehow the superficial cuts she made were not enough. She remembers, "Then I made one cut. . . . Real deep. I could see the fat under the skin. . . . I could actually see the end of the artery. . . . It was then that I realized just how bad the damage I'd inflicted on myself was. . . . And the scariest thing: It didn't hurt. Not at all. I mean, no pain. No burning."[37]

PUNISHING MYSELF

"Self-injury took seven years of my life; it was seven years of hell. It was a crutch, a burden, an excuse, a drug."—K.A., former self-injurer, age seventeen.

Quoted in Nancy L. Heath and Mary K. Nixon, "Concluding Comments from the Editors," in *Self-Injury in Youth: The Essential Guide to Assessment and Intervention*. New York: Routledge, 2009, p. 317.

Especially when self-injury becomes addictive, deeper and deeper wounds become necessary to soothe emotional pain. Then the risks of medical complications become very real. Jennifer, like most self-injurers, had not meant to cause real harm, but her deep cuts had gone too far. She tried to treat the injury herself and even went to school the next day, but after about twenty hours, she was getting weak and dizzy. She realized that she could not really stop the bleeding completely nor keep the wound closed. As eventually happens with many self-injurers in her situation, she had to go to the nearest hospital emergency room. There, her wound was cleaned and finally closed with thirty-one stitches. Her experience convinced Jennifer that her self-cutting had to stop. She wrote, "This can't keep happening. It just can't. That's all."[38] When people say that their self-injury does not hurt anyone, Conterio and Lader ask, "What about you, the self-injurer? *You* are important, and *you* are clearly getting hurt—emotionally as well as physically."[39]

Emotional Risks: Only a Temporary Fix

The risks of self-injury are indeed emotional as well as physical. When people say that they have to use self-injury as a survival tool, either to avoid suicide or to stop their emotional pain, experts point out that the coping tool does not really work. The emotional relief from self-injury does not last. The intense emotions return, and the self-injurer never learns how to cope with strong emotions or relieve tension and stress in healthy ways. That is why professionals consider self-injury to be a poor coping tool and self-destructive in the long run. Psyke.org explains,

> One of the problems with self-injury as a coping mechanism is that its effects are only temporary. Once the endorphins dissipate [fade away] and the consequences of hurting yourself become clear, you may experience feelings of guilt, shame, and remorse. Also, the negative feelings you experienced before hurting yourself may come back at this point or shortly thereafter. So, as a result of self-injury, you may feel even worse than you did before hurting yourself. And these negative emotions can be the beginnings of another act of self-injury.[40]

Self-injury has been called a temporary solution to a permanent problem. When it is used to block out negative emotions, it can seem like a "quick fix," but this solution stops people from dealing with their underlying pain. That is why Deb Martinson calls self-injury a "crude and ultimately self-destructive tool."[41] People do not heal the underlying emotional problems when they depend on self-injury. They do not rid themselves of the feelings of self-hate, shame, depression, helplessness, fear,

A Risky Form of Self-Injury

In 2008 doctors at the Nationwide Children's Hospital in Chicago reported that about 10 to 20 percent of teens who self-injure insert foreign objects under their skin. This is called self-embedding. The patients that the doctors saw had inserted things like unfolded paper clips, staples, and even pieces of crayons under their skin. This kind of self-injury is dangerous. William Shiels, one of the hospital doctors, says serious infections can result. He explains, "The infections aren't just at the site. You can get a deep muscle infection or a bone infection." If the embedded objects are not removed, they may also travel to other sites in the body, such as organs, and cause tears or other damage. Shiels says the risk of self-embedding as a form of self-injury is "significant."

Quoted in Tiffany Sharples, "Teens' Latest Self-Injury Fad: Self-Embedding," *Time*, December 11, 2008. www .time.com/time/health/article/0,8599,1865995,00 .html.

Of teens who self-injure, 10 to 20 percent do so by self-embedding, or placing objects under the skin.

tension, or any of the traumas or past experiences that they are trying to numb. They do not learn healthy coping tools.

Feeling Worse than Ever

Often, according to the Mayo Clinic, self-injury episodes increase the negative feelings that people have about themselves. The aftermath of a self-injury episode can be an increase in feelings of shame, guilt, and low self-esteem. This happens because self-injurers feel embarrassed and ashamed about the behavior. They may fear being "crazy" or "sick." They may hate themselves for losing control if they have been trying to resist self-injuring. They may feel sure that other people would judge them with disgust, horror, and shock. They may be disgusted with themselves for causing wounds and feel ugly because of the permanent scars. They often feel isolated and alone, unworthy of reassurance and support from friends or loved ones. Because of these feelings, many self-injurers become secretive with and withdrawn from the very people that they wish to be close to, love, and trust.

Damaging Relationships

The self-hate, loneliness, and loss of social connections are three of the biggest risks of self-injury. Drawing information from Tracy Alderman's book *The Scarred Soul*, the Self-Injury.net website explains that a big problem with self-injury is that it "keeps other people at a distance." According to the site, which quotes Alderman in this excerpt,

> self-injury encourages emotional distance from other people in several ways. First, "the secrecy and shame attached to many SI [self-injury] behaviors causes a lack of honesty and open communication between you and the important other in your life." You may have not told anyone about your self-injury. You may edit information about your self-injury and about how you feel (your emotional states.) You may even lie about what you do and how you feel. Each of these hinders or cuts off communication and intimacy with other people, which creates distance. You can't be close with others if you are lying to them."[42]

Self-injury encourages emotional distance from one's peers and cuts off communication and intimacy with others.

On another website for people with self-injury problems, several individuals describe their feelings of self-hate and the ways they feel cut off from other people. A girl identifying herself as Charlotte writes about her cutting, "I felt I had to punish myself, but now when I look at my scars and look back on what I did I feel so ashamed and angry with myself. I really hate myself sometimes, my cutting has left me a lot of scars many on my arms legs and stomach and I wish they were not there."[43] Other people on the site describe themselves as cowardly, weak, friendless, scared, or freakish for hurting themselves. Like many self-injurers, they say they wish for but cannot find sympathy and understanding. One teen writes anonymously on the website,

> I was at school today and I realised how much people don't understand how much people hurt and what they go through to go to the extent of cutting themselves, people saw the cuts all over my arm today and just said

things to me like "razorblade romance" and "sharpener blade warrior." It made me feel horrible. The feeling I had was horrible, I cried and my friends were asking me what was wrong. I couldn't even reply.[44]

"Outed"

Self-injury is almost always done in private, but eventually, most people who self-injure are either discovered or make the decision to tell someone else about the problem. Family or friends may see the wounds or scars. Medical treatment may be needed, so that hospital personnel question the nature of the injury. Or the self-injurer may find the burden of secrecy to be too great and confide in someone or ask for help. It is a risky, frightening time, both for the self-injurer and for the person who is learning about the problem. The person who self-injures is risking negative reactions. These reactions may isolate the self-injurer still further. Even when the reactions are supportive and loving, however, self-injury can cause pain and fear in other people.

Fifteen-year-old Jane was trying to keep her injuries a secret, but her boyfriend discovered her behavior after one bad cutting episode. It was a stressful moment. She says,

> The next time I saw my boyfriend I was wearing a long sleeve shirt to hide the cuts. I reached for something at his house, the sleeve pulled up, and a glimpse of red showed. He grabbed my wrist and forcefully I pulled away. The room went silent as he suddenly says nothing. He started asking questions and I didn't know what to say. I just wished that I could have disappeared. Staying in his room tears falling from my eyes all I could do was sit and stay quiet until he would accept me for my flaw. Someday I hope he understands, that everyone understands, why I am like the way I am.[45]

Rejection by Others

Jane wished for support and acceptance, but sometimes people who find out about self-injury are overwhelmed and react very

In Hospitals and Emergency Rooms

Doctors, nurses, and other medical personnel may have as difficult a time coping with self-injury as do family and friends. Some may react with horror, disgust, contempt, or hostility when a self-injurer requires treatment. Many self-injurers, forced to go to an emergency room for a wound, report very negative experiences. One twenty-eight-year-old woman says, "Many times [I've been] medically treated. Been stitched and stapled without anaesthetic. Had steri-strips on deep cuts that immediately came open and were then left. Been told off. Been told I was wasting people's time. Been told I was lying when I went back after the stitches came undone. Have been met with 'oh, my god!' when seeing my legs. Been lectured once how I shouldn't have done it." Another woman complains, "Of course several [doctors have been angry/abusive]—that's when they sew you up without a shot to deaden first. Like you deserve more pain [because you] do that to yourself. I wish there were more understanding and help out in the real world." Self-injury experts explain that reactions such as these are a common risk for self-injurers because of a lack of awareness, even in the medical profession, about self-injury. Experts, such as Deb Martinson and the researchers at Cornell University, are involved in outreach efforts to medical personnel to educate them about self-injury. Many physicians and nurses can be understanding and compassionate about self-inflicted wounds and treatment, but others have not yet learned enough about self-injury to be sensitive to their patients' needs.

Quoted in "In Their Own Words . . . ," SelfInjury.org. www.selfinjury.org/nsiad/quotes.pdf.

badly. Conterio and Lader explain, "Self-preservation is a basic instinct. Abandoning that instinct seems frightening, crazy, or at the very least counterintuitive to people who don't self-injure."[46]

In order to protect themselves from their negative feelings, some people can be very cruel. On a popular self-injury website, one high school girl who calls herself Summer says she was teased and bullied for her self-injuring behavior. She had told a couple trusted friends about it, but one of these friends told her boyfriend. At lunchtime one day he announced loudly,

"Summer cuts herself! . . . Look at the scars on her arms! Why do you think she wears all of those bracelets all the time?" In shame, Summer jumped up from the lunch table and ran, but the taunt followed her, "Where you goin' Scratchpad?" The cruel nickname and the story spread through the school. Summer was called "Scratchpad," "emo girl," "Scars," and "freak."[47] She says that she lost most of her friends, and many people stopped talking to her altogether.

REACH OUT, FREAK OUT

"You're trying to get people to know that you're hurting, and at the same time, it pushes them away."—Sarah Rodey, college student recovering from self-injury and bipolar disorder.

Quoted in Associated Press, "Self-Mutilation Rampant at 2 Ivy League Schools," June 5, 2006. www.msnbc.msn.com/id/13141254.

Even parents and family can be unsympathetic or cold about the need to self-injure. On one self-harm website, "Nikki" writes that her mother told her that cutting means something is terribly wrong with her and that "if anyone ever found out,"[48] she would be locked up in a mental institution. Another mother, when she found out about her daughter's self-injury, said, "When I learned that Alexis was cutting herself, I saw it as manipulative behavior and I wasn't going to succumb [give in] to it."[49] Other young self-injurers also report being told that they are just hurting themselves to get their way or "for attention." Alderman says that self-injury is definitely not an attention-seeking behavior. It is an attention-needing behavior, but what is needed is not criticism but caring, help, and support. Being labeled or threatened is one more risk faced by self-injurers when people find out about their wounds and scars.

The Pain of Others

Of course, most parents, family, and friends do want to help, and they are upset and hurt when they learn the secret. Alderman explains that initial reactions to self-injury include "shock and denial," "anger and frustration," "empathy, sympathy, and sadness," and "guilt."[50] The shock and denial happen because it is so hard for others to understand bypassing the safety catch and damaging oneself on purpose. As a result, people who learn about self-injury want to make the self-injurer stop and feel helpless and horrified when they cannot. They can also feel angry that the self-injurer

When they find out that their child is harming him- or herself, parents are usually shocked, angry, frustrated, sad, and, above all, guilty.

was deceiving them about the wounds and scars (for example, excusing wounds by saying they are due to cat scratches or falls or accidents). Family and friends may also feel that the behavior is somehow their fault. They worry that they did something to cause their loved one to self-injure, and they think that they have failed—as a parent, best friend, or even a good teacher.

One father, who calls himself James, has written about his feelings for his daughter who self-injured for years. He wrote, "My daughter cut herself again Wednesday, getting suspended by her school for bringing the knife to school, and getting busted for the cutting. Lots of emotions around this including ones of guilt, or that it is my fault. . . . She is in danger, I must protect her. But there is no tangible entity for me to attack. . . . The emotions are painful."[51] On a different blog, the daughter, Victoria, wrote about this time in her life, "It got really bad. But not only was it bad for myself, I was also harming my parents, my brother, my family, and my friends in ways I couldn't fathom until I finally stopped."[52] This family eventually recovered from the pain of self-injury, but before that happened, James went through the shock, guilt, sadness, and helplessness that Alderman describes. He lived with constant fear while his daughter remained unaware of how much he suffered for her.

People who care about a person who self-injures do feel fear. They are afraid of permanent injury or that the injury will escalate to suicide. They want desperately to make the self-injury stop. Sometimes this means, for a parent, trying to control the environment of a self-injurer. Parents may think that they should hide all the sharp implements in the house or watch over their child constantly so that he or she cannot self-injure. But fear is not good for relationships. Trust is lost, and the person who self-injures feels defensive, misunderstood, and belittled.

At the same time, many people who self-injure know how badly their loved ones hurt because of their behavior. Writing anonymously on a website, one girl describes her mother's pain. She says, "When I look into my mother's eyes these days, all I see is painful confusion like she's asking, 'How can she help me?'

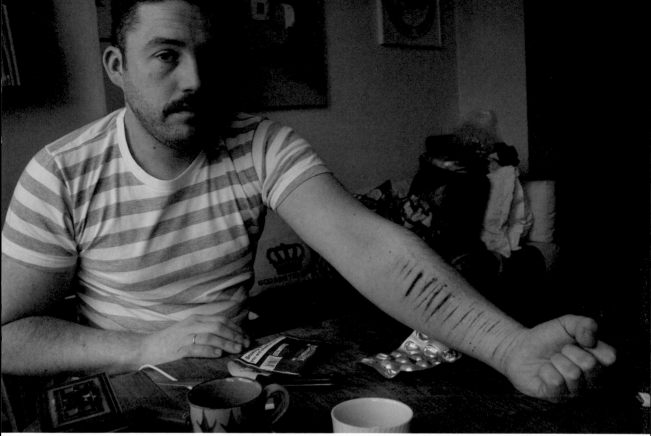

Unless the self-injurer makes the decision to stop self-injuring, counseling or family intervention can do little to stop it.

and 'How did this happen to my little girl?'"[53] This girl feels addicted and out of control. She wants to stop hurting her mother, but she cannot stop her self-injury.

Gordon Houghton, a British writer and former self-injurer, explains that people who love and care for someone who self-harms always have a difficult time coping. Because they do not know what to do, they can make the self-injurer feel worse. He describes a sixteen-year-old named Rachel who could not stop her self-injury behaviors. Houghton writes, "Rachel says her parents 'were scared by it. My dad gave me a lecture on God and took my blades away. My friends were scared too, though a few of them stepped into help. . . . But people trying to "fix" me only screwed things up more.'"[54] The pain they cause friends and family hurts self-injurers, and paradoxically may make them turn to self-injury even more because guilt, tension, and/ or anger increase.

To Escape Self-Injury

Houghton reminds everyone that the self-injurer would stop if only he or she knew how. Most self-injurers are scared and hurting, too. Wanting to stop and learning to do so are the only ways to reduce the risks of self-injury, but no one can stop the hurting unless the self-injurer makes the decision to stop. Even then, establishing good relationships, giving up self-injury, and recovering can be a long and difficult road, especially when self-injury feels like the only way to cope and survive.

CHAPTER 4

RECOVERY

No one knows the best therapy or treatment for self-injury. No one knows, for sure, how to persuade a self-injurer to want to stop. Professionals even argue about whether self-injury should be stopped when underlying issues have not been resolved. People who self-injure are individuals with different personalities, different problems, different diagnosed disorders, and different needs, so what works for one person may not help another. What experts and recovered self-injurers do know is that healing is possible. No one is doomed to live a life of self-injury, and people can recover when they make the decision to try.

Today, treatment methods and help programs emphasize respect for the self-injurer, learning healthy coping skills, non-judgmental exploration of emotional needs and issues, and compassion for the overwhelming feelings that can lead to self-harm. Some treatment programs involve hospitalization or residential treatment programs. Other self-injurers turn to outpatient therapy. Self-injurers also help each other with empathy and self-help tips through supportive Internet sites that fight for recovery. Karen Conterio and Wendy Lader, who run one kind of treatment program, offer this encouragement: "Everyone who has ever self-injured and stopped is eager to pass the message along about how this soul-destroying behavior can be overcome. Our patients' message is that the road to recovery is bumpy indeed, but is the best journey they ever took."[55]

The First Step of the Journey

Tracy Alderman says to people who self-injure, "First you need to want to stop. Without that, you won't be successful."[56] Recognizing that self-injury is a destructive tool and wanting to escape the cycle of repetitive self-injury is absolutely necessary for any treatment or therapy to work. Nobody can be forced to stop self-injuring against their will.

Conterio and Lader established the residential treatment programs named S.A.F.E. (Self-Abuse Finally Ends) Alternatives in Illinois, Missouri, and Texas and agree with Alderman. They say that treatment must be voluntary and that the self-injurer

A young woman is treated for her self-injury disorder at a S.A.F.E. Alternatives in-patient center. To be successful a S.A.F.E. patient must demonstrate a heartfelt and internal motivation to stop injuring.

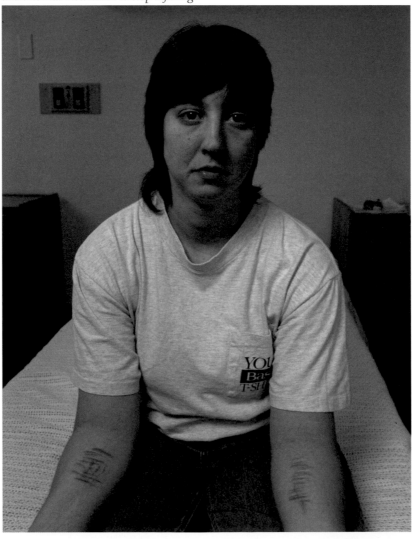

must be committed to change. They explain that "the patient must demonstrate a heartfelt and *internal* motivation to stop injuring. We screen out anybody who does not sincerely . . . want to get better and anyone who has arrived on our doorstep in response to an ultimatum from a relative, therapist, colleague, or friend."[57] This does not mean that the individual is sure he or she can change; he or she may be terrified, unsure how to survive without self-injury, and overwhelmed by the idea of giving up self-injury. However, the self-injurer needs to have come to a point of really wanting to stop.

Different people reach this point for different reasons, sometimes after years of self-injury. Victoria, for example, spent nine years self-injuring before she was ready to try to stop cutting at the age of seventeen. She was not only dependent on self-injury but also addicted to drugs. She made at least two suicide attempts. She was hospitalized for the suicide attempts and later spent eleven months in a juvenile detention center because of the drugs. She says, "However, I think I would have to say that self-injury was harder for me to overcome than my crack/cocaine addiction." The desire to stop self-injuring came slowly, but it finally came at a residential treatment program. She thinks, "Maybe it was because I wasn't ready yet and still had to hit a bottom, but I really don't know. Some things are just left [to] the unknown, I suppose. . . . However, the point is that I'm ready now. . . . I also threw myself into my recovery and came to the conclusion that I don't *ever* want to be that person I used to be."[58] When Victoria wrote those words in 2009, she had not self-injured for nine months.

Jennifer wanted to stop self-injury because the deep wounds she had accidently inflicted scared her. Justin Mills reached a point at which he felt hopelessness and "it was ingrained in my mind that cutting would progressively destroy my life."[59] Liz C. wanted to quit self-injuring when she realized that it did not calm and soothe her the way it used to do. Susan L. could no longer tolerate the feelings of hopelessness, guilt, and shame she experienced after self-injuring. Other self-injurers may be motivated by the pain and distress of loved ones and friends who insist that the self-injurer get help. Some decide to take the first step toward recovery when they find themselves missing work or school and unable to function in society because they self-injure so frequently. Many seek treatment when they find themselves frightened because self-injury no longer brings relief from intense negative emotions, and this situation triggers or increases suicidal thoughts.

Choosing Residential Treatment

Whatever the reasons for wanting to stop self-injuring, few people are able to do so without professional help, and residential programs are one way of getting that help. The S.A.F.E. Alternatives program, for example, admits people who live in the treatment center for about thirty days. The program's philosophy includes the idea that self-injury is both "futile" and "dangerous," that self-injurers can be empowered to help themselves, and that self-injury can be permanently cured. The S.A.F.E. website explains, "We also believe that self-injury is not an addiction over which one is powerless for a lifetime, people can and do stop injuring, with the right kinds of help and support. Self-injury can be transformed from a seemingly uncontrollable compulsion to a choice."[60] At S.A.F.E., staff members do not try to control the patients; instead, they try to help self-injurers to take responsibility for their own safety and stop feeling powerless and helpless.

A CRY FOR HELP

"Every time I went into the hospital, my plan was that somebody was going to take this hell away from me, and nobody ever did."—Alison, recovered self-injurer.

Quoted in Karen Conterio and Wendy Lader, *Bodily Harm*. New York: Hyperion, 1998, p. 296.

In order to make each individual responsible for his or her own choices, the S.A.F.E. program requires that each person sign a "No-Harm Contract." The contract demands that the person agree not to engage in any self-injury while in treatment.

Any violation of this contract leads to probation or dismissal from the program. Conterio and Lader admit that signing the contract is extremely difficult for many people. They may be afraid that they will get worse or "go mad" without their coping tool. Conterio and Lader say, "We remind patients that even though they may begin this time-limited undertaking with us, all their choices [such as resuming self-injury] are available to them when they leave. We do hope, however, that they will come to see and feel the rewards of life without self-injury."[61]

The S.A.F.E. Toolbox

In the S.A.F.E. program, participants explore the underlying reasons that they came to depend on self-injury and learn alternative ways to deal with and communicate their emotions, such as fear and anger. Treatment depends on using a "toolbox" with four major tools. The tools are:

- No-Harm Contract
- Impulse Control Log
- Five Alternatives
- Writing Assignments.[62]

The no-harm contract is usually individualized for each patient so that, together, the therapist and client work out the agreement. It always includes promising not to self-injure and to use the other three tools, but may also include agreeing to attend a substance abuse program if the patient has that problem or agreeing to work on an eating disorder if necessary or avoiding suicide attempts if the client is depressed and considering suicide. Since many self-injurers have problems with other self-destructive behaviors such as these, the S.A.F.E. program emphasizes healthy choices for the whole person.

Impulse Control Logs

The impulse control log is a kind of diary. Every time a person feels the impulse to self-injure, he or she writes down the self-injury urge and the thoughts and feelings that precipitated the urge. The person tries to identify what the self-injury episode would be communicating and what the outcome of the impulse was. For example, one S.A.F.E. patient, Ashley P., filled out an entry in her log like this:

> Self-injury thoughts: Cutting, burning, starving . . .
>
> Location: School cafeteria
>
> Situation: I was with a group of peers but on the outside.
>
> Feeling: Sad and lonely.
>
> What would self-injury accomplish? Scars, discharge [from the program because of the no-harm contract].
>
> What would I be trying to communicate with my self-injury? That I am lonely and wish I fit in better.
>
> Outcome: I . . . realized that my therapy might be able to help me learn how to get closer to people. . . . Being on the outside of things might be temporary.[63]

Five Alternatives

The five alternatives are a list of five (or more) comforting, soothing, or distracting activities that each patient chooses as alternatives to self-injury. Some possible alternatives include keeping a journal or writing in the impulse control log, listening to music, talking to a friend or counselor, taking a walk, or working on a hobby or craft project. Even though it is very painful to do, one important alternative is to sit quietly and experience one's feelings. This alternative helps people realize that the feelings will not drive them crazy or kill them, that they can feel uncomfortable without harming themselves, and that they can accept and tolerate negative emotions.

Writing Assignments

Finally, everyone in a S.A.F.E. treatment program is given fifteen writing assignments to complete. First, patients write an autobiography. Then, say Conterio and Lader, "The assignments focus on self-awareness, identification of feelings, family/relationship issues, and gender/body image issues."[64] The idea is to focus on exploring feelings, communicating thoughts, and making sense of why self-injury became a problem in the first place.

As part of the S.A.F.E. treatment program patients are given fifteen writing assignments, including an autobiography, that focus on exploring feelings and communicating thoughts.

All of the tools in the toolbox help people to stop and think when they get the desire to self-injure and to become empowered to resist their urges. As they succeed, they become confident that they can lead an injury-free life. At the same time that they are using their tools, people explore underlying feelings with their therapists and learn new coping strategies for their feelings of isolation, self-hate, shame, and powerlessness. They learn that they are not helpless and worthless at all. They learn to take responsibility for their own safety and to heal.

Success the S.A.F.E. Way

The S.A.F.E. Alternatives program reports that at least 75 percent of people who complete their treatment are injury-free after two years and that fewer than 10 percent of people drop out because of violating the no-harm contract. Many former self-injurers say that the S.A.F.E. Alternatives treatment program helped them recover when other therapies or hospitalizations failed.

S.A.F.E. also runs outpatient treatment programs and promotes long-term therapy for self-injurers after they leave a residential program to help them maintain an injury-free life. People in the outpatient program come for treatment during the day but go home at night. Often they meet in a group with other self-injurers who want to change, while seeing their own therapists to talk about and deal with individual problems and issues. They follow basically the same program as those in the residential program. They sign no-harm contracts and learn to use their toolboxes to keep themselves safe. Around the United States, various treatment facilities have adopted many of the S.A.F.E. treatment methods and made them available through clinics and outpatient hospital programs.

A Different Approach to Treatment

Many people have used the S.A.F.E. toolbox to take charge of their lives. However, the use of self-harm contracts is controversial. Studies have shown that no-harm contracts are of little value for people who are suicidal, and their value for people who self-injure is not accepted by everyone. Barent Walsh, for example, is an expert therapist who treats people who self-injure. He says, "I generally recommend *against* using Safety Contracts as a strategy to deal with self-injury, because they often have more risks than benefits."[65]

Walsh believes that such contracts just encourage people to keep their self-injury episodes a secret from their therapists. It is much too difficult, he says, to tolerate the emotional distress or feelings of emptiness without self-injury. Clients who self-injure after promising the therapist not to may feel like failures, feel misunderstood, and drop out of therapy. Their symptoms of psychological disorder may even get worse.

LEARNING RECOVERY SKILLS

"I can see the warning signs, like when I start to isolate myself, so I can stop the cycle before it starts."—Dawn, college graduate and recovered self-injurer.

Quoted in Jeanie Lerche Davis, "Self-Injury: One Family's Story," WebMD Feature, WebMD, p. 2. www.webmd.com/anxiety-panic/features/self-injury-one-familys-story.

He explains that people cannot give up the coping tool of self-injury until they have learned other, healthy coping tools that can replace the self-injury. Learning new coping tools can take a long time in therapy. Walsh urges other professionals, "*Do not ask self-injurers to give up the behavior before they are ready.*"[66] Many other therapists and clinicians agree with Walsh because in their own treatment experiences, they have discovered that restriction of self-injury behaviors has worsened emotional health or even led to suicide attempts in their patients.

Talk Therapy and Replacement Skills

Unless a client asks for a contract or is in serious danger from severe self-injury, Walsh believes in therapy that concentrates on resolving underlying emotional problems and teaching replacement skills instead of immediately preventing the self-injury. The idea is to make a gradual transition from self-injury behaviors to more healthy choices.

No one treatment method is known to work best for self-injury, so Walsh says that several different treatment methods may be useful for developing the ability to stop self-injury. Through talking with the therapist, the self-injurer may explore his or her thoughts and beliefs—such as whether he or she is

Talk therapy helps self-injurers explore thoughts and beliefs that may have led them to self-injure.

"bad," should feel shame, deserves punishment, is powerless and helpless, or is unlovable and worthless.

Other talk therapies might concentrate on the self-injurer's body image. People who have been sexually abused, for instance, might feel cut off from their own bodies, unable to accept their own sexuality, or feel ugly and unattractive as physical beings. These people might need body image therapy to learn to accept and feel good about their bodies.

People with post-traumatic stress disorder need to talk about and work through the trauma. Dissociation and flashbacks to the traumatic events are common problems for people with post-traumatic stress disorder. They may injure themselves to stop the flashbacks or "get back in touch with reality." Talk therapy involves not only learning different ways of coping other than self-harm but also providing a safe place for the patient to remember the trauma, since often traumatic details are not consciously remembered. The patient faces the bad memories, admits to him- or herself the fears and anger caused by the trauma, and is allowed to grieve about the past. Gradually, the traumatic events can be put in the past, and the person can appreciate being a survivor, learn to develop a positive self-image, and live in the present without being controlled by the need to avoid bad memories or the belief that he or she deserved the traumatic treatment.

In all of these therapies, however, new skills for dealing with intense emotions are a part of the treatment. Walsh says that nine types of replacement skills—strategies to use instead of self-injury—may be helpful for people. They are:

1. Negative replacement behaviors
2. Mindful breathing skills
3. Visualization techniques
4. Physical exercise
5. Writing
6. Artistic expression
7. Playing or listening to music
8. Communicating with others
9. Diversion techniques[67]

Calm and Relaxed

Some of these replacement skills are the same as those used by S.A.F.E. Alternatives, such as writing in a journal, talking to someone else, using music, exercise, art activities, or other distractions as chosen for an individual's "five alternatives." Mindful breathing and visualization, however, serve a different purpose. They are not distractions. They are to be used whether or not the person is thinking about self-injuring and are a way to practice reducing general stress in one's life. "Mindful breathing skills," says Walsh, "are often the most important in learning to give up self-injury."[68] Mindful breathing means concentrating on calm, relaxed breathing and not thinking about other things.

Walsh says that self-injurers are often so distressed that they are unable to focus and think clearly. They cannot let go of their

Sample S.A.F.E. No-Harm Contract

Every patient in a S.A.F.E. Alternatives treatment program signs a contract as one requirement of admission. This is one example of the kind of contract that might be used:

> As a candidate for the S.A.F.E. Alternatives program, I recognize that self-injury interferes with all aspects of my life. I am committed to treatment of my problem and to stopping all self-injurious behavior. I am aware of and agree to the following guidelines for my treatment:

1. No self-damaging or property-damaging behavior throughout my hospital stay. . . .

2. If I have a concurrent eating disorder, I agree to follow treatment recommendations to address this problem. . . .

3. Sexual contact with others, physical threats, assaultive behavior, stealing, use of nonprescribed drugs, or use of alcohol may lead to dismissal from the S.A.F.E. Alternatives program.

4. Elopement [running away] will automatically lead to discharge. . . .

(Patient signature and date)

(Witness signature and date)

Karen Conterio and Wendy Lader, *Bodily Harm*. New York: Hyperion, 1998, p. 297.

negative emotions and are overwhelmed by them. Walsh teaches his clients to practice slow, deep, in and out breathing while they say something silently inside their minds such as "Letting go of x."[69] The x can be anything, such as anxiety, perfectionism, anger, fear, or guilt.

When people are focused, calm, and relaxed, they can practice visualizing—or clearly imagining—peaceful, happy scenes, such as lying on an ocean beach or flying effortlessly through the sky like a bird. Visualization techniques like this are soothing and calming. The more calm and relaxed a person is, the less likely he or she is to need self-injury. Walsh practices visualization techniques with his patients during therapy sessions so that they can use these techniques alone at home whenever they are feeling stress and emotional turmoil.

Negative Replacement Skills

Negative replacement behaviors are a completely different way of dealing with emotional turmoil. They are ways of mimicking or pretending to self-harm without actually doing it. For example, instead of cutting to watch the blood flow, the person would

At a psychiatric unit for teenagers a young girl does a jigsaw puzzle as part of verbal, emotional, and body expression therapy aimed at monitoring and preventing crises such as depression, suicidal behavior, eating disorders, and self-abuse and injury.

draw on the skin with a red marker. Other negative behaviors include putting Ben Gay on the skin and feeling the tingle, briefly applying an ice pack to the skin, or stroking the skin with a soft brush and concentrating on the feeling. People can also draw a picture of the injury they want to perform or describe injuring themselves on a tape recorder. None of these activities actually damages the tissues, but they might feel real enough to satisfy the urge to self-injure. Walsh occasionally suggests negative replacement behaviors early on in therapy, before healthier techniques have been learned, but they are controversial among many therapists. Conterio and Lader, for example, are firmly opposed to negative replacement behaviors. They argue that such techniques keep people focused on self-injury and preoccupied with hurting themselves. S.A.F.E. forbids negative replacement behaviors in its program because they believe it may increase the urge for actual self-injury.

Walsh agrees that negative replacement behaviors might "cue actual self-injury because [they] are so similar to the real thing."[70] But he argues that the behaviors can help some people to make the transition from self-injury to healthy replacement techniques. For example, Walsh tells the story of a client he calls Nikki. She would cut a grid of marks into her arms using an X-acto knife. Her negative replacement behavior was to use the X-acto knife to cut exactly the same pattern into layers of construction paper. She said that this activity helped her to avoid self-injury several times during the beginning of her therapy. Later, she learned healthier coping skills and dropped the negative replacement behavior.

Does Medication Help in Treatment?

While people are in therapy for self-injury and learning replacement skills, some professionals use medication to help clients control self-injury urges and focus on recovery. Although no medication has been developed to stop self-injury, certain psychological disorders can be eased with the appropriate medication. For example, a person who self-injures and suffers from depression might be given antidepressant medication. Antianxiety medication might be used for people with anxiety disorders.

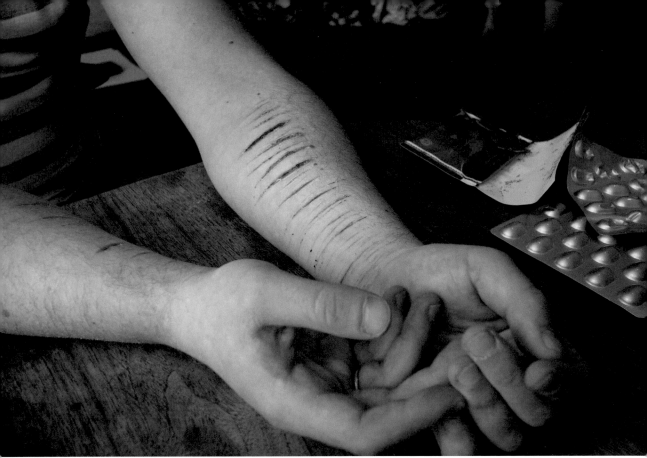

Medications for depression and anxiety are sometimes used for self-injurers, but S.A.F.E. believes the drugs mask emotions and should be used as little as possible.

Medications can improve mood and increase motivation in therapy, but few studies have shown that they can reduce self-injury behaviors. At S.A.F.E., the philosophy is that medications mask feelings and should be used as little as possible. S.A.F.E. wants patients to feel their emotions and learn to deal with them rather than to ease the emotions with medication. Other experts believe that a combination of medication for psychological disorders and therapy works well for people who self-injure.

Some researchers have wondered whether self-injury is a physical addiction like alcoholism or drug addiction. With these addictions, drugs are sometimes used that can block the effects of the abused drugs. The theory is that if the addictive substance provides no reward or good feeling, the person will stop craving it. A drug that blocks the effects of opiates (such as heroin or morphine) on the brain is called an opiate blocking agent. One such drug, Naltrexone, has helped people recover from opiate addiction and has helped alcoholics. It blocks the endorphins, which are natural opiates produced by the brain, too. If self-injurers use their behavior to increase stress-soothing endorphins in their brains, perhaps opiate blockers could reduce self-injury episodes. Naltrexone has stopped self-injury in some people who harm themselves as a result of autism or mental retardation, so researchers have studied Naltrexone with people who have borderline personality disorder and also self-injure. The results have not been completely positive. Naltrexone and other opiate blockers have reduced self-injury in some people with BPD and other disorders, but have not changed behaviors at all in other studies. Research is still ongoing, but at present, no appropriate medication has been identified for self-injury addictions.

Self-Help Toward Recovery

Even though no perfect therapy or "magic pill" for self-injury exists, most people can and do recover with a combination of courage, determination, support from professionals, and self-help. On the Internet, for example, people turn to other self-injurers for understanding, encouragement, and tips for dealing with their self-harm behaviors. At websites dedicated to helping people who self-injure, members share personal stories, support each other, and report recovery successes to encourage others.

Psychologists Craig D. Murray and Jezz Fox of the University of Manchester in England conducted a study of one self-harm Internet discussion group in 2006. The researchers interviewed forum participants and concluded that the group helped many members to reduce the severity and frequency of their self-injury. It enabled people to make social connections, to feel understood, and to get emotional support at any time of the day or night that they needed help.

Internet support groups enable members to learn from each other how to help themselves. At the United Kingdom's National Self Harm Network (NSHN), for instance, participants post long lists of distractions to try when the urge to self-injure is strong. What works for one person may not work for another, but everyone can see all the ideas and try a suggestion that seems appealing. Some of the contributed distraction suggestions include "throwing socks against a wall," "ripping up paper into small pieces," "popping bubble wrap," "rubbing body lotion on where you want to hurt yourself," "organising your room, clothes, photographs," "playing with play dough or modelling clay," "watching a candle burn," and "dressing up, glamorous or silly."[71] The forum members at NSHN work to break the self-destructive cycle of self-injury, whether or not they have "real world" therapy or treatment. They are determined to help themselves.

In the United Kingdom the National Self Harm Network's program had participants list various ways they distract themselves when they have the urge to self-harm. Among them is popping bubble wrap.

It Can Be Done

Most people who self-injure do find the strength to end their self-destruction, although the process may take years. People may try several different treatments before they find the approach that works for them; they may successfully recover and then relapse during a period of stress and harm themselves again. But with continued effort, a large majority finds that the desire to self-injure does go away and that they have healed. Walsh says,

> My work with self-injurers has taught me, again and again, that great things are possible from those who are able to transform pain into affirmation. The life stories of self-injurers often move from anguish, isolation, and bodily harm to accomplishment, affiliation [positive relationships], and self-protection. We professionals are fortunate to play some role in assisting these seekers to find a higher ground.[72]

PREVENTION OF REPETITIVE SELF-INJURY

In May 2010 Dallas, Texas, eighth-grade teacher Faith Davis Johnson wrote a newspaper article expressing her concerns about the growing incidence of self-injury in school populations. She was worried that schools do not have the information and training available to deal with the problem. She pointed out that very few schools around the country had programs available either to try to prevent self-injury or to intervene appropriately and helpfully with students just beginning to experiment with self-injury. Johnson believes that schools should be able to provide support for all students and is frustrated that so little is being done to tackle the issue of self-injury. Yet this situation does not exist because school personnel do not care. It exists because research into self-harm is just beginning, and experts are not yet sure what kinds of prevention programs might work best to address the problem.

Prevention and Risk Factors

Self-injury research experts and clinicians acknowledge that they cannot even accurately diagnose repetitive self-injury, much less identify all the causes and risk factors involved or predict which people might become addicted to self-injury. So how can they know which prevention efforts will work? According to the Cornell Research Program on Self-Injurious Behavior, "Virtually nothing has been written on effective ways of preventing the adopting of self-injurious practices. Indeed, this is an area badly in need of research."[73] No one knows for sure how to prevent self-injury, but Cornell researchers, along with other experts, are trying to address the problem.

Family problems can add psychological stresses that lead teens to engage in self-destructive behaviors as a way of coping.

The Cornell researchers, as well as other researchers around the world, look at what is known about some of the reasons people begin to self-injure, and they consider the risk factors that might trigger self-injury experimentation. They consider such factors as psychological disorders, emotional distress, the role of the media, contagion among groups of people, and the need for others to know what to do when someone begins to experiment with self-injury. Then they suggest several possible prevention strategies that might be useful.

Interventions at Schools

Two of the strategies identified by the Cornell program include increasing "social connectedness" and paying attention to "stress in the external environment."[74] Social connectedness is about the support of family, friends, and school. Stresses in the external environment might include problems such as bullying at school or family problems at home. Instead of feeling socially connected, people who self-injure often report feelings of loneliness, isolation, and invisibility. Family problems may include abuse, neglect, or trauma, but they may also be stresses such as a divorce, a death in the family, or the chronic illness of a parent. Psychological reactions to stresses and lack of connectedness can lead to self-destructive behavior as a coping mechanism. Self-destructive behaviors are risky actions that may include eating disorders and substance abuse, which are common behaviors in people who self-injure, too.

Although no one knows how to predict who will turn to self-injury, experts do believe that supportive programs for people at risk could reduce all self-destructive behaviors. Because so many people who begin to self-injure are school-age, Cornell researchers and other experts suggest that school interventions aimed at helping students reach out to others and teaching healthy coping strategies could reduce self-injury in children and teens.

The SEYLE Study

In 2010 the European Union began a large, long-term research study to test the usefulness of different preventive methods for risk-taking and self-destructive behaviors. These behaviors include alcohol and drug use, self-injury, suicide attempts, aggression, depression, anxiety, and involvement in other dangerous situations. The project is named Saving and Empowering Young Lives in Europe (SEYLE). It involves eleven thousand teens in schools in eleven different countries. In different schools, the researchers are testing the value of three different kinds of interventions to reduce self-destructive behaviors. In some schools, the researchers are providing "gatekeeper training" for teachers and school staff. This means school staff are trained to recognize students engaging in at-risk behavior. The teachers are taught how to ask questions about an individual student's behavior, persuade the individual to seek or accept help, and refer the student to an appropriate helper, such as a therapist, counselor, or hospital. School staff are provided with cards listing appropriate sources of help in the community.

In other schools, the researchers are providing professional screening services to identify at-risk students. They give questionnaires about lifestyles and psychological problems to all the students in the school. Then, students who test as having mental health problems, self-destructive behaviors, or high risk-taking behaviors are interviewed by a psychiatrist or psychologist to determine whether they need intervention. Students with social problems (for instance, bullying or isolation) are encouraged to join a healthy lifestyle group, such as scouting clubs or sports activities. Those with depression, anxiety, phobias, substance abuse, nonsuicidal self-injury, or suicidal thoughts are referred for professional treatment.

A COORDINATED EFFORT

"There is no sure way to prevent self-injury. Prevention strategies may need to involve both individuals and communities, including parents, schools, medical professionals and coaches, for instance."—Mayo Clinic Staff.

Mayo Clinic Staff, "Self-Injury/Cutting: Prevention," Mayo Clinic. www.mayoclinic.com/health/self-injury/DS00775/DSECTION=prevention.

In still other schools, researchers are conducting awareness training for all the students. The researchers explain, "The awareness intervention is designed to promote knowledge of mental health, healthy lifestyles and behaviors among adolescents enrolled in the SEYLE project."[75] Every participating student is given a booklet that provides self-help advice and the names and phone numbers of counseling facilities and healthy lifestyle groups. Over a four-week period, the students learn about and discuss mental health issues, how to recognize depression and crisis and stress situations, and how to help a friend who is at risk. Posters about mental health and giving and accepting help are hung in each classroom. During discussion groups, the students are involved in role-playing sessions in which they act out

As part of the SEYLE program some schools give questionnaires to students to find out about lifestyle and psychological problems any may have.

conflicts and explore healthy ways to resolve them. They practice healthy coping skills when, for instance, they are having a conflict with a teacher, parent, or friend. They explore how to react when they are under stress or during a crisis. The researchers hope that these activities help teens know what to do to resolve problems.

At the end of the SEYLE study in December 2011 the researchers will begin the process of reevaluating all the student participants to see what intervention works best. They hope to have clear, scientific evidence of which kinds of school-based programs might help to reduce and prevent self-destructive behaviors in teens, including self-injury.

School Support Groups

In the United States Matthew D. Selekman, a social worker and expert on self-injurers, believes that schools can help prevent self-injury with early identification of people who are just beginning to experiment with self-harm. Rather than including all the school's students in an educational and awareness program as does SELYE, he suggests that school faculty can learn to "red-flag" or respond to clues that an individual student is experimenting with or thinking about self-injury. This approach is recommended by many experts who are concerned that whole school educational programs might encourage contagion or experimentation. Selekman says that teachers and others can be taught to be alert for self-injury signs (such as wearing long-sleeved clothing in summer or displaying wounds) and then respond with compassion and an offer to help. He warns that too many adults react to signs of self-injury with "disgust, anxiety, or fear." School personnel have to be taught not to lecture or demand information; instead, they have to be "available for emotional connection, support, and advice when needed."[76]

With the Stress-Busters' Leadership Group some schools teach coping skills to at-risk teens. When they complete the program, the teens help others who are at-risk for self-harm.

Then, for at-risk students who are experimenting with self-harm, Selekman has developed an intervention called the Stress-Busters' Leadership Group. This is a school-based support group that teaches coping skills to teens who self-harm. The group is run by a counselor and assisted by students who have completed the program and want to help others. Selekman says, "Over nine sessions, students look at their strengths and 'protective shields'; learn skills related to mindfulness, meditation, loving kindness, and compassion toward self and others; focus on finding balance and harmony in their lives; learn how to navigate family minefields; and acquire effective tools for mastering school stress."[77]

Preventing Contagion

Selekman's approach to prevention targets individual at-risk students instead of the whole school population, in part because he believes that self-harming epidemics are a risk in schools. The Cornell Research Program also explains that whole-school education about self-destructive behavior can "backfire" and encourage emotionally vulnerable teens to try the very behavior that educators are trying to reduce. The Cornell researchers say that just teaching people about what self-injury is, why people do it, and how dangerous it is actually can cause an increase in experimenting with self-injury. Prevention of this kind of self-injury contagion is the goal of many experts who advise schools to avoid teaching about self-injury to everyone and to prevent self-injuring students from displaying their injuries to other students.

Barent Walsh also suggests that schools have to have strategies in place to prevent self-injury from spreading among teens. He says that schools first have to identify the individual who is self-injuring and refer him or her to a specific "point person," such as the guidance counselor or school nurse. The point person then must explain to the self-injurer that it hurts their friends and other students to talk about self-injury. Self-injuring students should be encouraged to talk to point persons or therapists but asked not to talk about self-injuring to peers because such talk is "triggering" for vulnerable people. Also, Walsh recommends, "Students [should be] asked not to appear in school with visible wounds or scars as these visible reminders are also very triggering. . . . Some students may need to have extra sets of clothing in school to cover wounds or scars."[78]

Many educators and professionals assume from practical experience that self-injury is contagious and that prevention efforts should focus on contagion, but scientific studies have shown no evidence that contagion is real. Nevertheless, one self-help website suggests to people who want to stop self-injuring, "Try not to spend time with others who self-injure or engage in self-destructive lifestyles. Self-injury sometimes has a 'contagious' quality to it, and your behavior might be triggered by the company of others who are harming themselves."[79] Because of this "contagious quality" some experts do not approve of the idea of group counseling for self-injuring people. These experts argue that self-injurers can be involved in groups that teach coping skills or aim to improve self-esteem, but they should not discuss self-injury behaviors in the group. Such talk can trigger self-injury episodes in other group members.

Student-to-Student Interventions

Despite concerns about contagion, however, self-injury professionals recognize that peers and friends are often the first people to know when someone begins to self-injure. Cornell researchers say, "As such, peers constitute the 'front line' in detection and intervention."[80] Usually, friends and peers do not want to imitate the self-injurer but are worried, perhaps horrified, and desperately want to help. One approach to helping young people help someone who self-injures is called The Signs of Self-Injury Prevention Program. The program consists of an educational DVD and discussion kit designed for high school students that teaches how to recognize signs of self-injury and how to respond to an individual in need of help. It is based on a similar program for suicide prevention developed by the nonprofit organization Screening for Mental Health. That program has been scientifically studied and shown to reduce suicide risk in young people.

The Signs of Self-injury program teaches the ACT® method of intervention to high school students. ACT® stands for acknowledge, care, and tell. *Acknowledge* means that students

When Mistakes Happen

First Signs, a British organization dedicated to helping people who self-injure, recognizes that sometimes prevention means avoiding danger and getting medical help. Its website advises:

> It is very important that you tell someone if you have hurt yourself severely or if you have taken an overdose/swallowed chemical substances. It is normal to be scared, but it is essential to get proper medical attention as quickly as possible. The following bullet points give some situations where medical attention should be sought; however it is not exhaustive.

- If the wound continues to bleed heavily once you have [tried first aid], including bandaging;

- If the cut is deep and has exposed underlying muscle, this is dark red in colour and may look like a slab of meat;

- If you have lost sensation in the area of injury, or more widespread; you may have damaged a nerve;

- If a burn is on a sensitive area of the body (e.g., face), over a joint or on the palm—the healing process creates scar tissue that can shrink the skin, causing potential movement difficulties for life;

- If a burn is severe, or large in area;

- If a burn is caused by chemicals;

- If after a few hours or several days you can see the wound is infected; it could be red, sore, swollen or weeping.

FirstSigns.org, "First Aid for Self-Injury and Self-Harm." www.firstsigns.org.uk/help/first-aid.

learn to acknowledge the signs of self-destructive behavior instead of ignoring them, take the signs seriously, and be willing to listen to the person's feelings. *Care* is demonstrating concern and understanding, reassuring the self-injurer that he or she is not alone, and expressing worry for the friend or loved one who self-injures. *Tell* means to tell a responsible, trusted adult who can get the individual the help and treatment he or she needs.

The Signs of Self-Injury Prevention Program can help friends help friends or a self-injurer to recognize what to do to help him- or herself. It has not yet been studied like the Signs of Suicide Prevention Program because it is so new, but experts hope that it will have the same positive effect of reducing self-injuring behavior in young people.

Self-Injury and the Media

Prevention of self-injury may depend on educating young people about the way the media can influence people's behavior, too. Cornell researchers theorize that news stories, songs, and celebrity talk about self-injury may be one cause of experimentation with self-injury, especially for teens. The researchers say, "Helping adolescents and young adults become critical consumers of

Cornell researcher Janis Whitlock believes that some teens may respond to media stories about self-injury by trying the behavior.

media may lessen their vulnerability to adoption of glamorized but fundamentally poor coping strategies."[81] Graphic news images of people's self-injuries can also be triggering for people who are fighting to avoid self-injury. Although no one is sure that teaching young people to reject the "fad" of self-injury can really prevent it, some researchers believe that some instances of self-injury might be prevented by school discussions of the effects of the media on society's view of what is "normal." The idea that the media can increase the incidence of self-injury is called "social contagion." It is not peers who trigger the contagion but the larger society.

Janis Whitlock explains, "Since the 1980s, references to NSSI [nonsuicidal self-injury] in media stories and popular culture have risen sharply, and may be contributing to an increase in prevalence."[82] Studies of other kinds of self-destructive behavior have determined that the media affect what young people will try. Whitlock says,

> Although we can never . . . know whether media has influenced the spread of self-injurious behavior, many studies have shown that media do play a significant role in the spread of related behaviors such as suicidality, violence, and disordered eating. . . .
>
> The Internet may be another vector for social contagion since it serves as a platform for hundreds of message boards, YouTube videos, and social networking sites where individuals with a history of or interest in self-injury provide informal support or share ideas.[83]

Self-Injury and the Internet

Caitlin Scafati was fourteen years old when she began searching for sites on the Internet where she could find support for her self-injury and her eating disorder. Caitlin was overweight, teased at school, socially isolated, and depressed. She found sites on the Internet that encouraged her to starve herself into thinness and to cut herself to cope with her feelings of worthlessness and pain. Members on some discussion boards offered tips about cutting and talked about self-injury as just a lifestyle choice. Caitlin felt understood and accepted by the anonymous people on the boards. She read about celebrities, such as Princess Diana and Fiona Apple who had admitted injuring themselves, and these stories, she said, "made it seem cool and OK."[84] Unlike reputable self-injury sites that are dedicated to helping self-injurers, the sites Caitlin found harmed her and made cutting seem "hip" instead of an unhealthy way to cope. Fortunately, Caitlin told her parents about her self-injury when she was fifteen, and they got her into counseling.

Caitlin is an adult now and has recovered from both her self-destructive behaviors. She knows the sites she visited were dangerous and has stayed away from them for many years. They taught her dependency on her self-destructive behavior and did nothing, in the end, for her emotional pain. Whenever possible, Internet servers such as Yahoo and AOL shut down sites like the ones Caitlin found, but still, people sometimes find chat rooms and journals that encourage self-destruction rather than help them to heal.

BEING THE GOOD FRIEND

"Remember you're not responsible for ending the self-abuse. You can't make your friend stop hurting himself or get help from a professional. The only sure thing you can do is keep being a good friend."—Mental Health America, advice for friends of self-injurers.

Mental Health America, "Factsheet: Self-Injury." www.nmha.org/go/information/get-info/self-injury.

In the United Kingdom, Oxford University researchers did a study of young people who self-injure and discovered that one out of five had first learned about the behavior online. For example, seventeen-year-old Danielle, of Belfast, Ireland, says, "I think the Internet played a major role; I think it started off my self-harm. I was already thinking about it so [I] went to the web to find out more. I just typed 'self-harm' and there were

Self-Injury Is Not Cool

In interviews, Angelina Jolie has been open about injuring herself as a teen, but she is upset that some interviewers have made it seem as if her self-injury is something to admire or imitate. She explains, "I was just . . . a kid. I was like 13. And, I was saying that it is not something that is cool. It's not cool. And I understand that it is a cry for help." Jolie does not self-injure now and does not encourage others to do it, but she remembers what happened after one interviewer wrote a story that made her self-injury seem "interesting":

> And then I met somebody who said they'd seen movies of mine and then showed me where they had cut themselves. I had to explain, first off, not to do that. But it made me really . . . angry at the people who represent me in a way that would get that person to do that and show me. I don't understand why people would want to use something so damaging. It's like, let's make me look "cool" and worry a lot of people in my family.

Quoted in Self-Injury.net, "Famous Self-Injurers." http://self-injury.net/media/famous-self-injurers.

In interviews actress Angelina Jolie has been outspoken about her incident of self-injury when she was thirteen. She understands it was a cry for help and warns teens that self-injury "is not cool."

hundreds of videos. Some are good but others can be very damaging. If I see a picture [of cuts], it can encourage me to do it."[85]

The British Royal College of Psychiatrists urged in 2010 that all websites should remove any material that might trigger self-harm. It says that too many sites glorify or glamorize self-injury. Sites such as YouTube have many thousands of videos about self-harm and cutting. British psychiatrist Margaret Murphy explains, "The kinds of things we are worried about are the graphic videos of self-harm [injuries] that are posted to sites like YouTube. Young people tell us that images can trigger memories and that makes them much more likely to self-harm."[86] The British doctors have asked all website owners to link directly to websites that offer professional help on pages where videos or discussions of self-injury encourage the behavior.

YouTube does take down any self-injury videos that frankly urge other young people to self-injure, but, like other Internet sites, it does not forbid all videos of self-harm. The idea is that people should be free to discuss issues and post videos that are honest communications about social problems. Although banning material about self-injury from the Internet might prevent some instances of repetitive self-injury, Google, the owner of YouTube, says that it must maintain a balance between safety and free speech. In the end, avoiding material that triggers self-harm or experimentation is up to each individual. Whitlock, Conterio, and Lader suggest that clinicians explore with their clients whether they should avoid Internet use that could trigger or encourage self-injury. The Mayo Clinic recommends that school education about the sometimes negative influence of media might reduce the the risks of experimentation for all young people. The Royal College of Psychiatrists has called for better training for teachers about the problem and dangers of self-injury so that they can learn to deal effectively with students who experiment with hurting themselves or have become addicted to the behavior. Former self-injurers recommend that other young people stay away from any Internet material that makes self-injury seem acceptable or that triggers the urge to self-harm. However, individuals who find themselves drawn to self-injury cannot be completely protected by avoiding media representations of the behavior. True prevention of self-injury is about each troubled individual and means, says Lader, "dealing with the real issue—their out-of-control emotions."[87]

Prevention One Act at a Time

Professionals and self-injury experts do not know with certainty how to prevent self-injury nor can they control society's messages, but every person who self-harms can strive to prevent the behavior for him- or herself. A British newsletter titled *Self-Harm Overcome by Understanding and Tolerance (SHOUT)* offers

Hundreds of videos on the Internet feature people injuring themselves. Evidence indicates that the videos can cause other people to engage in the behavior.

affirmations—caring, positive messages—to help people stop hurting themselves. *SHOUT* suggests that these affirmations could be useful to remember for anyone who is trying to prevent personal acts of self-injury:

> My feelings are real and important and need to be listened to.

> There are good reasons for the pain I feel. But it doesn't have to last forever. I deserve to have the support I need to get over the things that have hurt me.

> When I feel bad or guilty or dirty, that's how I have been made to feel by things that have happened in my life. It's not the truth about me.

> I am a real, worthwhile, good person who deserved to be respected and cared about.

> In my heart of hearts, I know what I feel and what I need. I can trust and respect myself. I can stand up for what is right for me.

> I have suffered more than enough in my life. I can have some kindness now. I don't deserve to be hurt anymore."[88]

Introduction: A Troubling Problem

1. American Self-Harm Information Clearing House (ASHIC), "Mission." www.selfinjury.org.

2. Quoted in Laura A. Dorko, "Literature Review: Development of a Website for Educators Addressing How to Understand, Recognize, and Respond to Student Self-Injury," Educators and Self-Injury, 2009. http://educatorsandselfinjury.com/literature-review.

3. Deb Martinson, "Self-Injury: Beyond the Myths," fact sheet, National Self-Injury Awareness Day, March 1, 2002. www.selfinjury.org/nsiad/factsht02.pdf.

4. Deb Martinson, "Self-Help: Organized and Otherwise," Palace.net. www.palace.net/~llama/psych/fself.html.

5. Quoted in Deb Martinson, "How Do You Feel About Stopping, Either a Session or Forever?" Self-Injury: You Are NOT the Only One, Palace.net. www.palace.net/~llama/psych/quot.html.

Chapter 1: Harming Oneself

6. Quoted in Elizabeth E. Lloyd-Richardson, Matthew K. Nock, and Mitchell J. Prinstein, "Chapter 3: Functions of Adolescent Nonsuicidal Self-Injury," in Mary K. Nixon and Nancy L. Heath, eds., *Self-Injury in Youth: The Essential Guide to Assessment and Intervention*. New York: Routledge, 2009, p. 30.

7. Quoted in Lloyd-Richardson et al., *Self-Injury in Youth*, p. 31.

8. Quoted in Karen Conterio and Wendy Lader, *Bodily Harm: The Breakthrough Healing Program for Self-Injurers*. New York: Hyperion, 1998, p. 134.

9. Mary K. Nixon and Nancy L. Heath, "Introduction to Nonsuicidal Self-Injury in Adolescence," in *Self-Injury in Youth*, p. 4.

10. Elana Premack Sandler, "Self-Injury: Addiction? Parasuicide? Cry for Help? Or None of the Above?" *Psychology Today*, July 2, 2009. www.psychologytoday.com/blog/promoting-hope-preventing-suicide/200907/self-injury-addiction-para suicide-cry-help-or-none-the.

11. Tracy Alderman, "Tattoos and Piercings: Self-Injury?" The Scarred Soul (blog), *Psychology Today*, December 10, 2009. www.psychologytoday.com/blog/the-scarred-soul/200912/tattoos-and-piercings-self-injury.

12. Laura, "My Self-Harm Story," The Site.org. www.thesite.org/community/reallife/truestories/selfharm.

13. Quoted in Michelle Eisenkraft, "Self-Injury: Is It a Syndrome?" *New School Psychology Bulletin*, vol. 4, no. 1, 2006, pp. 122–23.

14. Quoted in "What Is Borderline Personality Disorder? *DSM-IV-TR* (2004) Criteria for Diagnosis of Borderline Personality Disorder," Borderline Personality Disorder Resource Center, New York–Presbyterian University Hospital of Columbia and Cornell. http://bpdresourcecenter.org/DSM-IV.html.

15. American Psychiatric Association, "Non-Suicidal Self Injury," proposed revisions, *DSM-5* Development. www.dsm5.org/ProposedRevisions/Pages/proposedrevision.aspx?rid=443.

16. Patrick L. Kerr, Jennifer J. Muehlenkamp, and James M. Turner, "Nonsuicidal Self-Injury: A Review of Current Research for Family Medicine and Primary Care Physicians," *Journal of the American Board of Family Medicine*, vol. 23, no. 2, 2010, pp. 240–59. DOI: 10.3122/jabfm.2010.02.090110. www.jabfm.com/cgi/content/full/23/2/240.

17. Quoted in *Science Daily*, "True Extent of Self-Harm Amongst Teenagers Revealed," September 4, 2008. www.sciencedaily.com/releases/2008/09/080903101414.htm.

18. Michael Eddleston, M.H. Rezvi Sheriff, and Keith Hawton, "Deliberate Self Harm in Sri Lanka: An Overlooked Tragedy in the Developing World," *British Medical Journal*, vol. 317, July 11, 1998, pp. 133–35. www.bmj.com/cgi/content/extract/317/7151/133.

Chapter 2: The Causes of Self-Injury

19. Sarah Michelle Fisher, "Self-Mutilation: Introduction," Personal Stories, Psyke.org. www.psyke.org/articles/en/self-mutilation.

20. Quoted in Conterio and Lader, *Bodily Harm*, p. 61.

21. Quoted in Conterio and Lader, *Bodily Harm*, p. 63.

22. Quoted in Conterio and Lader, *Bodily Harm*, pp. 67–68.

23. Quoted in Conterio and Lader, *Bodily Harm*, p. 82.

24. Quoted in Conterio and Lader, *Bodily Harm*, p. 78.

25. Quoted in "Etiology (History and Causes)," Self-Injury: You Are Not the Only One, Palace.net. www.palace.net/llama/psych/cause.html.

26. Digby Tantam and Nick Huband, *Understanding Repeated Self-Injury*. New York: Palgrave Macmillan, 2009, p. 96.

27. Tantam and Huband, *Understanding Repeated Self-Injury*, p. 32.

28. Matthew K. Nock, "Self-Injury," *Annual Review of Clinical Psychology*, vol. 6, 2010, p. 351. www.wjh.harvard.edu/~nock/nocklab/Nock_ARCP_2010.pdf.

29. Tracy Alderman, "Myths and Misconceptions of Self-Injury: Part II," The Scarred Soul (blog), *Psychology Today*, October 22, 2009. www.psychologytoday.com/blog/the-scarred-soul/200910/myths-and-misconceptions-self-injury-part-ii.

30. Justin Mills, "The Art of Bloodletting," Personal Stories, Psyke.org. www.psyke.org/articles/en/art.

31. Cornell Research Program on Self-Injurious Behavior in Adolescents and Young Adults, "What Do We Know About Self-Injury?" Cornell University Family Life Development Center. www.crpsib.com/whatissi.asp.

32. Janis L. Whitlock, Jane L. Powers, and John Eckenrode, "The Virtual Cutting Edge: The Internet and Adolescent Self-Injury," *Developmental Psychology*, vol. 42, no.3, 2006. www.crpsib.com/documents/Dev%20Psych%20Dis.pdf.

33. Nock, "Self-Injury," p. 356.

Chapter 3: The Risks of Self-Injury

34. Conterio and Lader, *Bodily Harm*, pp. 228–35.

35. Barent W. Walsh, *Treating Self-Injury: A Practical Guide*. New York: Guilford, 2008, p. 22.

36. NursingTimes.net, "Self-Injury," February 23, 2009. www .nursingtimes.net/whats-new-in-nursing/self-injury/ 1995882.article.

37. Jennifer, "My Trip to the E.R.," Personal Stories, Psyke.org. www.psyke.org/cgi-bin/search/search.pl?q=emergency%20 room%20stitches&showurl=%2Fpersonal%2Fj%2Fjennifer %2Findex.html.

38. Jennifer, "My Trip to the E.R."

39. Conterio and Lader, *Bodily Harm*, p. 228.

40. Psyke.org., "Self Injury FAQ." www.psyke.org/faqs/self injury/#sec7.

41. Deb Martinson, "Introduction," Self-Injury: You are NOT the Only One, Palace.net. www.palace.net/~llama/psych/ injury.html.

42. Self-Injury.net, "Talking About Self-Injury with Others. http://self-injury.net/information-recovery/recovery/talking-about-self-injury-others.

43. Charlotte, "Untitled," Personal Stories, Psyke.org. www .psyke.org/personal/c/charlotte.

44. Bleeding Teen, "Why Don't They Understand?" Personal Stories, Psyke.org. www.psyke.org/personal/b/bleeding_ teen.

45. Jane, "I Didn't Cheat," Personal Stories, Psyke.org. www .psyke.org/personal/j/jane/46.

46. Conterio and Lader, *Bodily Harm*, p. 229.

47. Self-Injury.net, "Scratchpad," Personal/Recovery Stories. http://self-injury.net/creativity/personal-stories?page=1.

48. "Nikki," Living with Self-Injury, Personal Stories, Psyke .org. www.psyke.org/history/200210/personal/living/nikki/.

49. Quoted in Conterio and Lader, *Bodily Harm*, p. 33.

50. Tracy Alderman, "Helping Those Who Hurt Themselves," *Prevention Researcher*, vol. 7, no. 4, 2000, pp. 5–8. www .parenting.cit.cornell.edu/documents/Helping%20 those%20who%20hurt%20themselves.pdf.

51. James, "Being a Dad Through Self-Injury," MereWisdom .org, January 12, 2009. http://merewisdom.org/2009/01/self-injury.

52. Victoria, "Survival of a Self-Injurer," Delicate Melody, March 17, 2009. http://delicatemelody.com/survival-of-a-self-injurer/comment-page-1/#comment-91.

53. IfTearsWereRed1, "Mommy's Kisses," Personal/Recovery Stories, Self-Injury.net. http://self-injury.net/creativity/personal-stories/mommys-kisses#more.

54. Gordon Houghton, "Secret Shame Part 2," eNot Alone, p. 2. www.enotalone.com/article/2995.html.

Chapter 4: Recovery

55. Conterio and Lader, *Bodily Harm*, p. 295.

56. Tracy Alderman, interview by Bob McMillan, "Self-Injury," transcript from online Concerned Counseling conference, March 3, 1998. www.cyc-net.org/reference/refs-self-mutilation-alderman2.html.

57. Conterio and Lader, *Bodily Harm*, p. 213.

58. Victoria, "Survival of a Self-Injurer."

59. Mills, "The Art of Bloodletting."

60. S.A.F.E. Alternatives, home page. www.selfinjury.com.

61. Conterio and Lader, *Bodily Harm*, p. 215.

62. Conterio and Lader, *Bodily Harm*, p. 247.

63. Quoted in Conterio and Lader, *Bodily Harm*, p. 256.

64. Conterio and Lader, *Bodily Harm*, pp. 259–60.

65. Walsh, *Treating Self-Injury: A Practical Guide*, p. 121.

66. Walsh, *Treating Self-Injury: A Practical Guide*, p. 122.

67. Walsh, *Treating Self-Injury: A Practical Guide*, p. 127.

68. Walsh, *Treating Self-Injury: A Practical Guide*, p. 129.

69. Walsh, *Treating Self-Injury: A Practical Guide*, p. 134.

70. Walsh, *Treating Self-Injury: A Practical Guide*, p. 129.

71. NSHN Forum, "Distractions That Can Help," National Self Harm Network. www.nshn.co.uk/forum/index.php?topic=16069.0.

72. Walsh, *Treating Self-Injury: A Practical Guide*, p. 274.

Chapter 5: Prevention of Repetitive Self-Injury

73. Cornell Research Program on Self-Injurious Behavior in Adolescents and Young Adults, "What Do We Know About Self-Injury?"

74. Cornell Research Program on Self-Injurious Behavior in Adolescents and Young Adults, "What Do We Know About Self-Injury?"

75. Danuta Wasserman et al., "Saving and Empowering Young Lives in Europe (SEYLE): A Randomized Controlled Trial," *BMC Public Health 2010*, vol. 10, no. 192, April 13, 2010. www.biomedcentral.com/1471-2458/10/192.

76. Matthew D. Selekman, "Helping Self-Harming Students," *Health and Learning*, vol. 67, no. 4, December 2009/January 2010, pp. 48–53. www.ascd.org/publications/educational_leadership/dec09/vol67/num04/Helping_Self-Harming_Students.aspx.

77. Selekman, "Helping Self-Harming Students."

78. Barent Walsh, "Some Basic Features of a School Protocol to Manage Self-Injury and Prevent Contagion," Cornell Research Program on Self-Injurious Behavior in Adolescents and Adults. www.crpsib.com/documents/SchoolProtocolToManageSI.pdf.

79. Deb Martinson, "How Can I Help Myself?" Self-Injury: You Are NOT the Only One, Palace.net. www.palace.net/llama/psych/selfinjury.html.

80. Cornell Research Program on Self-Injurious Behavior in Adolescents and Young Adults, "What Do We Know About Self-Injury?"

81. Cornell Research Program on Self-Injurious Behavior in Adolescents and Young Adults, "What Do We Know About Self-Injury?"

82. Janis Whitlock, "The Cutting Edge: Non-suicidal Self-Injury in Adolescence," Research Facts and Findings, ACT for Youth Center of Excellence: A Collaboration of Cornell University, University of Rochester, and New York State Center for School Safety, p. 4. www.actforyouth.net/documents/NSSI_Dec09.pdf.

83. Whitlock, "The Cutting Edge."

84. Quoted in Mary Fischer, "Thrills That Kill," *Readers Digest*, February 2006. www.rdasia.com/thrills_that_kill.

85. Quoted in BBC Radio Newsbeat, "Young People Self-Harming with Sharp Objects Up 50%."

86. Quoted in BBC Radio Newsbeat, "Young People Self-Harming with Sharp Objects Up 50%."

87. Quoted in Fischer, "Thrills That Kill."

88. Psyke.org, "Affirmations for People Who Self-Harm," 2002, reprint from *Self-Harm Overcome by Understanding and Tolerance (SHOUT)*. www.psyke.org/history/200210/coping/af firmations.

Chapter 1: Harming Oneself

1. Do you think repetitive self-injury is a symptom of a psychological disorder, or should it be considered a diagnosis in itself?

2. Is a person who chooses extreme tattooing or multiple piercings a self-injurer? Why or why not?

3. If you bite your nails or pick at a scab, is that self-injury? Is everyone, at some level, a self-injurer?

Chapter 2: The Causes of Self-Injury

1. What are some of the emotional reasons that people turn to repetitive self-injury?

2. Why do some researchers suggest that self-injury is an addiction similar to drug use?

3. What life experiences might make someone with good, loving parents feel powerless and uncared for?

Chapter 3: The Risks of Self-Injury

1. What are some physical risks of self-injury?

2. What are some emotional risks of self-injury?

3. What are some of the reactions that family and friends tend to go through when they find out a person is self-injuring?

Chapter 4: Recovery

1. Are no-harm contracts valuable tools, ineffective strategies, risky ploys, helpful agreements, or worthless documents? Why?

2. Which treatment methods do you think would be most successful in helping self-injurers recover?

3. What distraction or skill do you think might best help a person avoid self-injuring?

Chapter 5: Prevention of Repetitive Self-Injury

1. Do you think self-injury is a problem in your school? Should the school be addressing the issue? Why or why not?

2. Provide some arguments for and against the idea that self-injury can be contagious. Are you at risk?

3. If a friend or loved one admitted to you that he or she was self-injuring, what should you say or do? Would it be easy or hard to respond with compassion and calm?

ORGANIZATIONS TO CONTACT

American Self-Harm Information Clearing House (ASHIC)
521 Temple Pl.
Seattle, WA 98122
phone: (206) 604-8963
e-mail: ashic@selfinjury.org
website: www.selfinjury.org

ASHIC was established by Deb Martinson to raise awareness about self-injury and provide education to people who self-injure, their friends and families, and medical professionals. Its main project is the National Self-Injury Awareness Day.

Mental Health America
2000 N. Beauregard St., 6th Floor
Alexandria, VA 22311
phone: (800) 969-6642
crisis phone: (800) 273-8255
fax: (703) 684-5968
website: www.mentalhealthamerica.net

Formerly known as the National Mental Health Association, this organization's mission is to educate the public about mental health, fight for equal and appropriate mental health care for all people, and provide support to people living with mental health issues or substance abuse problems.

National Alliance on Mental Illness (NAMI)
3803 N. Fairfax Dr., Ste. 100
Arlington, VA 22203
phone: (703) 524-7600
information helpline: (800) 950-6264
fax: (703) 524-9094
website: www.nami.org

NAMI is a national nonprofit outreach, educational, and advocacy organization dedicated to improving the lives of people with mental illnesses and their families.

National Self Harm Network (NHSN)
PO Box 7264
Nottingham NG1 6WJ
United Kingdom
phone support helpline: 0800 622 6000
e-mail: info@nshn.co.uk
website: www.nshn.co.uk

NHSN provides information and support for people who self-injure and their families throughout the United Kingdom and internationally. It offers a moderated forum for self-injurers at its website, as well as educational materials and support through its helpline and e-mail.

Self-Abuse Finally Ends (S.A.F.E.) Alternatives
University Behavioral Health
2026 W. University Dr.
Denton, TX 76201
phone: (800) 366-8288
e-mail: info@selfinjury.com
website: www.selfinjury.com

S.A.F.E. offers inpatient and outpatient treatment, referrals and lectures, blog, and educational materials about self-injury.

Books

Susan Bowman and Kaye Randall, *See My Pain! Creative Strategies and Activities for Helping Young People Who Self-Injure*. Chapin, SC: Youthlight, 2006. Written for caregivers and youth counselors, this book presents practical tips and activities for learning communication skills, distractions, writing about feelings, and other alternatives to self-injuring.

Jan Kern, *Scars That Wound, Scars That Heal: A Journey Out of Self-Injury*. Cincinnati, OH: Standard, 2007. Written with a religious perspective, the real-life story of Jackie follows her journey from self-injury and emotional pain to recovery and healing. (This book contains graphic descriptions and could be triggering for some people.)

Peggy J. Parks, *Self-Injury Disorder*. San Diego: ReferencePoint, 2010. Explores the causes and demographics of self-injury, current research, and treatment.

Lawrence E. Shapiro, *Stopping the Pain: A Workbook for Teens Who Cut & Self-Injure*. Oakland, CA: Instant Help, 2008. This is a workbook for teens, complete with many activities, that helps people understand why they self-injure, control the urges to self-harm, and find better, healthier coping skills.

Mary E. Williams, ed., *Self-Mutilation*. Introducing Issues with Opposing Viewpoints: Detroit: Greenhaven, 2009. This book presents different viewpoints on whether self-injury is a problem, why people engage in the behavior, and what should be done about the problem of self-injury.

Websites

Befrienders Worldwide (www.befrienders.org). This international website offers support in thirty-nine countries to people who are depressed, lonely, or despairing, with the goal of decreasing the risk of suicide by providing someone to listen. Support is offered by e-mail or hotlines. Most are available twenty-four hours a day.

RecoverYourLife.com (www.recoveryourlife.com). One of the largest virtual support communities for self-injury on the Internet, Recover Your Life offers chat rooms, live help, a discussion forum, and advice for people who self-injure. It is a strong pro-recovery site.

Samaritans (www.samaritans.org/talk_to_someone.aspx). This volunteer organization is based in the United Kingdom. Anyone can call, e-mail, or write to Samaritans volunteers to talk about any emotional stress at any time of the day or night. Samaritans volunteers are not professionals but offer caring support, nonjudgmental listening, and a chance to explore feelings and options. Phone calls incur charges, but e-mail and letters are free. Confidentially is always maintained.

Secret Shame: SelfHarm.net (www.selfharm.net). Established by Deb Martinson, this large site provides detailed information about self-injury and its causes, as well as self-help, first-aid, and treatment advice.

INDEX

PICTURE CREDITS

Cover: Eduard Harkonen/Shutterstock.com

© bildgentur-online/begsteiger/Alamy, 31

© Catchlight Visual Services/Alamy, 51, 55, 78, 82

© David Grossman/Alamy, 65

© Emilio Ereza/Alamy, 75

© eStock Photo/Alamy, 18

Fred Prouser/Reuters/Landov, 89

© FR Images/Alamy, 81

Gale/Cengage, 25, 28

Hossein Fatema/EPA/Landov, 45

© imagebroker/Alamy, 12, 86

© Janine Wiedel Photolibrary/Alamy, 8, 49, 57, 73

Jim Varney/Photo Researchers, Inc., 20

© Jon Arnold Images Ltd/Alamy, 35

Lewis J. Merrim/Photo Researchers, Inc., 68

© Michael Ayre/Alamy, 27

Paul Shlykov/Shutterstock.com, 37

PHANIE/Photo Researchers, Inc., 16, 71

© redsnapper/Alamy, 91

© Robin Beckham @ Beepstock/Alamy, 33

Stephen Ferry/Getty Images, 23

Terry Whitaker/Photo Researchers, Inc., 41

Time & Life Pictures/Getty Images, 60

ABOUT THE AUTHOR

Toney Allman holds a BS in psychology from Ohio State University and an MA in clinical psychology from the University of Hawaii. She currently lives in rural Virginia and writes books for students on a variety of topics.